AUBERGE DU CHOCOLAT

The secrets of fine chocolate making

AUBERGE DU CHOCOLAT

The secrets of fine chocolate making

New Holland

This paperback edition published in 2013
First published in 2011 by
New Holland Publishers (UK) Ltd
London • Cape Town • Sydney • Auckland

Garfield House, 86–88 Edgware Road,
London W2 2EA, United Kingdom
www.newhollandpublishers.com

Wembley Square First Floor Solan Road Gardens Cape Town 8001 South Africa
Unit 1, 66 Gibbes Street, Chatswood, NSW 2067, Australia
218 Lake Road, Northcote, Auckland, New Zealand

ISBN 978 1 780094595

Senior Editor: Lisa John
Photographer: Edward Allwright
Production: Laurence Poos
Design: Penny Stock
Publisher: Clare Sayer

10 9 8 7 6 5 4 3 2 1

Reproduction by Modern Age Repro House Ltd, Hong Kong
Printed and bound by Toppan Leefung Printing Ltd (China)

This book contains chocolates made with raw eggs. It is prudent for pregnant or nursing mothers,
invalids, the elderly, babies and young children to avoid uncooked eggs. This book also includes
chocolates made with nuts and nut derivatives.

Contents

All about chocolate

Chocolate has been eaten and enjoyed for hundreds of years. Understanding more of its intriguing history and the processes by which it is made can only enhance your enjoyment of making and eating it.

The History of Chocolate

The history of chocolate is full of myths and mystery and sometimes it can be hard to separate fact from fiction. What follows are generally perceived to be the basic facts.

FOOD OF THE GODS

The earliest records we have of chocolate date back some 1500–2000 years ago in the Central American rainforests. Here we find the *Cacao* tree, worshipped by the Mayan civilization. *Cacao* is Mayan for 'God Food', which later gave rise to the modern generic Latin name of *Theobroma cocoa*, being 'Fruit of the Gods'. Although we might agree with the sentiment behind the name, this is certainly not a form of chocolate that we would recognize today. The Mayans produced a spicy, bitter-sweet drink made by roasting and pounding the cocoa beans and then adding maize and capsicum. This was then left to ferment. This very special drink was used in religious ceremonies and by the very wealthy. It is also thought to be something only men were allowed to drink, as one of the properties attributed to the drink was that it was a powerful aphrodisiac. It was thought that allowing women to drink it would give them all manner of ideas above their station.

The cocoa bean also held significance for the Aztecs. Unfortunately, their climate and land did not lend itself to the cultivation of cocoa trees and this may have given the beans an even higher value. Beans were used as a currency and it is reported that 100 beans could buy you a slave.

As they were unable to grow the beans, the Aztecs obtained them through trade or the spoils of war. As well as needing the beans for currency, the Aztecs made a similar drink to the Mayans. Like the Mayan *Cacao,* the Aztec *Xocolat* was linked with religion and the supernatural. According to legend, their creator and god of agriculture *Quetzalcoatl* arrived on a beam of the morning star, carrying a cocoa tree from Paradise. Wisdom and power came from eating the fruit of the tree. The value given to *Xocolat* can be seen in the description of the drink by Emperor Montezuma, who reportedly drank *Xocolat* 50 times a day: he is supposed to have said that the divine drink 'builds up resistance and fights fatigue. A cup of this precious drink permits a man to walk for a whole day without food.'

MORE THAN JUST A DRINK

In 1519 the Spanish conquistador Henri Cortes found cocoa beans while ransacking Aztec treasure stores. He realized the beans had commercial value and took them to Spain where a drink more suitable for the European palate was eventually produced by mixing the powered roasted beans with sugar and vanilla. Chocolate remained highly valuable and its origins were kept secret in Europe for almost a century. So much of a secret that in 1579 when some English buccaneers boarded a Spanish treasure galleon and found what looked like 'dried sheeps' droppings', rather than the gold and silver they'd expected, they set fire to it in frustration. Traders in Europe eventually discovered Spain's secret and chocolate soon became available throughout Europe.

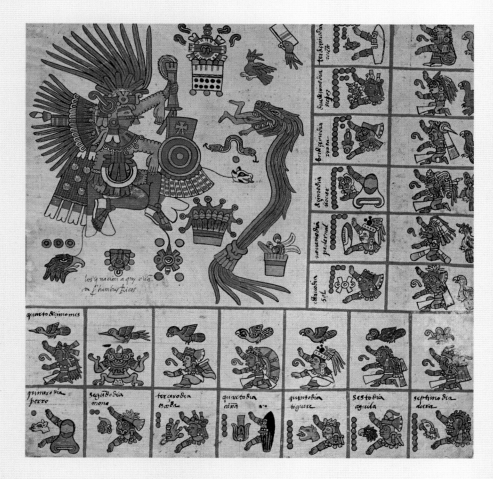

LEFT The Mayans made a chocolate drink by pounding the beans from a cocoa pod.

RIGHT Shown here top left, Quetzalcoatl is often depicted holding a cocoa bean or cocoa tree.

In 1520 chocolate arrived in England and it rapidly became all the rage. In 1657 London's first chocolate house, the 'Coffee Mill and Tobacco Roll', opened and the new chocolate drink quickly became a bestseller. Clubs built up around the drinking of chocolate and many a business deal was conducted over a cup. Chocolate houses were in effect the forerunners of today's popular coffee houses. As chocolate became more sought after, politicians imposed an excessive duty of 10–15 shillings per pound (comparable to approximately ¾ its weight in gold). This made chocolate very much a luxury item and therefore something to be enjoyed by the aristocracy and the business community. It was nearly 200 years before this duty was dropped.

FROM DRINK TO MILK CHOCOLATE BAR

The next main event was the production of the first chocolate bar. In 1828 Dutch chemist Johannes Van Houten wanted to make a smoother, more palatable chocolate drink so invented a process to remove the cocoa butter from the cocoa beans. This paved the way for production of chocolate as we know it today. In 1847 the Fry & Sons factory in Bristol, a family-run business that had been making chocolate since the mid-18th century, used the Van Houten process to add sugar and cocoa powder to the extracted cocoa butter and were thus the first to produce a chocolate bar fit for widespread consumption. In 1875 Daniel Peter, a Swiss manufacturer, then further developed the chocolate bar by adding milk powder to the mix, thereby creating the first milk chocolate. Earlier attempts to make a milk chocolate had used liquid milk but this did not combine well with the other ingredients and soon turned rancid. Peter, after years of experimentation, was in the end inspired by his neighbour Henri Nestlé's invention of condensed milk, which Peter used to make milk drinking chocolate, and *farine lactée*, a milk food he used to feed his own daughter.

LEFT Chocolate houses sprang up all over Europe selling a popular chocolate drink. This was eventually sold to make at home.

RIGHT The first chocolate bar was produced in the mid-19th century and changed the way the public enjoyed chocolate.

How Chocolate
is made

All chocolate starts life as a cocoa pod. Although cocoa pods come in various colours, shapes and sizes, most are the size and shape of 25–30 cm (10–12 in) rugby ball. These are cut from the tree, slashed open, the flesh scooped out and the many small fruits piled onto a plantain leaf mat. Here they are left to ferment for up to seven days, depending on their quality, in order to take on their chocolatey flavour. Ideally, they are then left in the sun to dry but in a rainforest climate, roll-on covers can be used, or the fruits can be dried in an oven, a process that unfortunately can affect the flavour of the chocolate. The farmer will then sort and bag his crop and sell it to international buyers.

ROASTING AND SEPARATING

The conditions under which the cocoa is grown affect the taste of the final chocolate but so do the processes used at factories. The beans are roasted at 120–140°C (250–275°F) for long enough to bring out their wonderful intense flavour but not so long that they end up burnt. This is where the skill of the roaster comes in. The outer layer of the bean is then removed (and used in gardens as ground cover and decoration), in a process called winnowing. This leaves behind the cocoa nibs.

FAR LEFT Cocoa pods are cut open to reveal a fleshy interior, containing many fruits or cocoa beans.

LEFT Once dried and roasted, the outer layer of the bean is removed to leave cocoa nibs.

BELOW In order to achieve a fine-quality chocolate, the chocolate must be conched.

Cocoa nibs are finely milled to create cocoa liquor, some of which is then pressed to extract cocoa butter, leaving behind a solid mass called cocoa presscake. This presscake undergoes further processes in order to produce cocoa powder.

MIXING AND CONCHING

One of two processes then occurs depending on exactly what type of chocolate is being made. Ever since Hershey discovered how to remove cocoa butter from chocolate in order to make it more suitable for soldiers' ration packs in the Far East during the Second World War, we've had two types of chocolate. The first is made very quickly. It takes only about 12 hours to make: the cocoa butter is removed and replaced with hydrogenated vegetable fats. The second type, valued among chocolate connoisseurs, undergoes a much longer process. Cocoa butter is added to the cocoa liquor, along with sugar and, in the case of milk chocolate, powdered milk. The chocolate is then passed through granite rollers at about 50–80°C (120–180°F) in a process known as conching, which is a kneading and smoothing process. The fineness of the chocolate is determined by how long it remains in the conch. The resulting chocolate melts in the mouth without leaving a cloying taste and is considered a far superior product to the chocolate produced using vegetable fats.

Where Chocolate is grown

Cocoa is grown in a band of 26° either side of the Equator. The trees won't just grow anywhere; they require constant warmth and rainfall. Even this won't work if there is not enough shade and nutrients. Approximately 70 percent of the world's cocoa beans come from Africa – the Côte d'Ivoire alone produces about 1.4 million tons of beans a year.

TYPES OF COCOA BEAN

Most of the African beans, however, are a common type of bean known as Forastero, which are grown

for bulk, not quality. Ghana is the world's second-largest producer of cocoa beans with over 600,000 tons per year. Cocoa is also grown in Indonesia, Brazil, Venezuela, Ecuador, Togo, Mexico and Papua New Guinea and other Latin American countries and in the Caribbean. Generally the cocoa beans grown in Latin America and the Caribbean are considered to be better quality, although some very good beans come from Africa. Traditionally the most flavoursome beans are of the type known as Criollo. They are red, elongated, somewhat fragile beans with flavours of raspberries and citrus. These account for less than 5 percent of cocoa production. In the eighteenth century a hurricane caused natural cross-pollination of the Criollo and Forastero beans, giving rise to a hybrid called Trinitario with a great flavour of apples, oak and balsam. This bean and other hybrids can produce excellent flavour and robustness.

SINGLE-ORIGIN AND SINGLE-ESTATE CHOCOLATE

Where the cocoa is grown, the weather conditions, the soil and the farming methods all affect the taste of the beans produced – rather like the concept of *terroir* in wine. As people become more and more excited about

LEFT Different types of cocoa bean are grown to satisfy demand either for bulk or for quality.

RIGHT Cocoa is grown in a band close to the equator, where the need for warmth and rainfall is easily met.

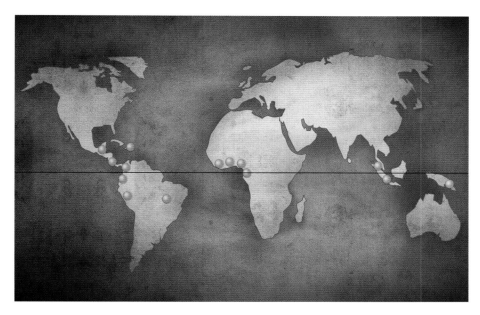

quality chocolate, there is a movement towards eating more single-origin and single-estate chocolate; that is chocolate made from beans grown in one particular area or plantation. As you get more involved in discovering and devising your own chocolate recipes, you might also like to experiment with this.

CHARACTERISTICS OF SINGLE-ESTATE CHOCOLATES

You may wonder if chocolate tastes any better if made from single-origin or even single-estate beans. Taste is, of course, a personal thing but the big difference you will notice is the complexity of flavour. As with wine, you will taste different flavour notes and levels. This increase in complexity will obviously increase the depth and excitement of your chocolates.

For example, if you are making a tangerine truffle or ganache then it could be worth experimenting with using a Madagascan coverture. The Madagascan coverture has light citrus flavours a bit like tangerine. Or try using Ecuadorian coverture, which has jasmine flavours. If you want something really fruity use a couverture from Venezuela, as this evokes the flavours of ripe red plums and dark cherries.

Other single-origin flavours you might like to try are those from Trinidad and Tobago, which are fruity but with spicy, often cinnamon, flavours. Jamaican chocolate is usually bright and fruity with a subtle pineapple flavour.

Another great way to use single-origin chocolate is simply on its own. It is excellent made into thins for the perfect end to a meal (see pages 122–125 for method).

Every single-origin chocolate tastes different so do experiment to find your favourites and to make your chocolate-making more interesting.

BLIND TASTING

If you are having fellow chocoholics round then it could be fun to do your own blind tasting of single-origin chocolates. Buy small amounts of six different single-origin chocolates from a chocolatier and put them in containers simply labelled 1–6. The packaging may have some notes about the tastes and origins but you could also ask the chocolatier. Then invite your guests to see if they can work out what flavours they recognize from the chocolate, where the chocolate is from and what percentage of cocoa solids are present. It is fun and very enlightening. It might also give you some ideas for how to use the chocolates in future recipes.

Chocolate techniques

Making chocolate requires a few essential skills. But don't panic, all of these techniques are easily learned. Start with the basics and gradually build up – provided you can temper chocolate, you can make wonderful treats and, more importantly, have fun doing so!

Tempering chocolate

To get a crisp snap and even shine, chocolate needs to be tempered. Chocolatiers can sometimes be guilty of implying that tempering is some extremely complex operation. It isn't, but as with all things it does require practice. People often assume, wrongly, that tempering means bringing the chocolate to a specific temperature. This is not the case and, in order to understand what tempering does, it is helpful to think about what chocolate is.

If you looked at chocolate under a microscope you would see lots of cocoa butter crystals of the same size fitting neatly together. It is this that gives the chocolate a crisp snap and shiny finish. In order to work with chocolate you have to melt it and as soon as you melt it, the butter crystals move around. As chocolate cools, its cocoa-butter content can solidify into different crystalline configurations, which leaves the cooled chocolate with a disordered crystalline structure – no longer the neat rows fitting snugly together. The chocolate takes on a mottled and matte appearance and a weak structure, which causes it to crumble rather than snap when broken. So, if we simply melt chocolate and use it to coat ganache and other fillings, when it sets (and this will take a long time), the chocolate will be dull, grey, grainy and soft.

One crystalline form in particular is the strongest and most stable and has the best texture and shiniest finish. Tempering encourages 'seeds' of this particular type of crystal to form and causes the other types of crystal to melt. The favoured crystals then multiply throughout the chocolate as it cools, once again arranging themselves so they fit neatly together.

The factors involved in tempering are time, movement and temperature and it is the correct interaction of these factors that will result in beautifully tempered chocolate. All of this makes tempering sound like a complex process but it is actually rather easy to achieve. Tempering machines can be bought but are only useful if you plan to temper vast quantities at any one time, otherwise it is best done using one of the three following methods.

For the tabling and seeding methods (see pages 19 and 20), you need to start by melting the chocolate (see box below). Do not melt chocolate in a bain-marie or over a pan of boiling water. If you melt chocolate in this way you are very likely to get water into your chocolate and ruin it. You also shouldn't melt chocolate in a pan over direct heat, as you'll inevitably burn it, which also renders it unusable.

For the microwave method (see page 21), start with chocolate pellets, or chocolate that has been chopped into small pieces.

Melting chocolate

Use one of two methods to melt chocolate. For both, use chocolate pellets or chop chocolate into small pieces. Either heat the chocolate in a very low oven (about 50°C/122°F) for about 5 minutes, or in a microwave for 30 seconds at a time, stirring between each heating. Stirring will help to melt any lumps and make sure that all the chocolate is heated evenly. It is important that you don't overheat the chocolate – if you do it will be totally useless and all you can do is throw it away.

Tabling method

This is the classic way of tempering chocolate but it is hardly used today, as it is very time-consuming and requires a marble bench. It is, however, the most spectacular way of tempering and is used in demonstrations for that reason.

1 Melt the quantity of chocolate you need (see opposite). Pour approximately two-thirds of the melted chocolate onto the marble slab.

2 Use a large, flexible scraper (available from DIY shops) to repeatedly pull the chocolate together and then spread it out. This causes the chocolate to cool quickly and to thicken. The chocolate now contains a number of 'seed' crystals. As the chocolate temperature drops, more crystals form. Plain chocolate should be about 31–32.5°C (87–90.5°F); check this by putting a tiny piece of the chocolate on your bottom lip. If it feels cool, it's ready. Milk chocolate and white chocolate should reach 29–30.5°C (84–86.9°F).

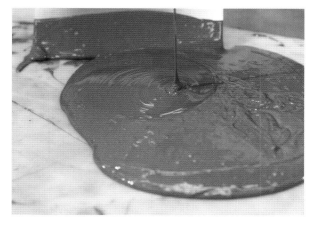

3 Once the required temperature is reached, quickly stir in the remaining third of the melted chocolate. This will melt or stabilize any unstable crystals. If this doesn't work, it is possible that there are not enough 'seed' crystals in the first two-thirds (for example, if the chocolate hasn't been cooled enough) or the remaining third is too hot. Unfortunately, should this be the case you will have to start all over again. When tempered, transfer the chocolate to a bowl ready for use.

Seeding method

This method is fast and easy. Chocolate is melted and then small pieces of solid chocolate, known as 'seed' chocolate are gradually added to it and stirred until no more can be melted.

1 Melt about two-thirds of the chocolate you need (see page 18). Once melted, it will contain no crystals.

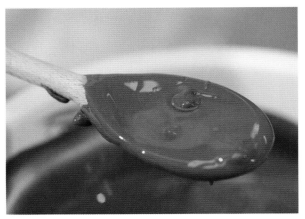

2 Add the remaining unmelted chopped chocolate or pellets bit by bit, stirring all the time. This final third is full of crystals and is being used to 'seed' the liquid chocolate. When no more solid chocolate will melt into the liquid, the chocolate is tempered.

How can I check the chocolate is tempered?

As tempering is so important it is worth checking you have fully tempered your chocolate. As you become more expert, you will know just by feel and appearance that the chocolate is tempered but before you reach that stage here is how to test it. Put a small amount of your tempered chocolate onto a piece of greaseproof paper. If the chocolate sets quickly with a lovely shine, it is tempered.

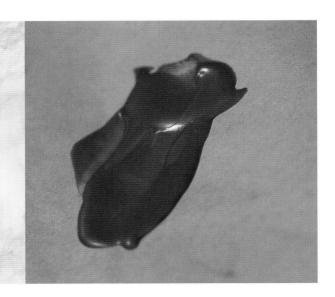

Microwave method

This method is ideal for tempering small quantities of chocolate quickly – in other words perfect for the amateur or home chocolatier. It requires a bit of patience and elbow grease at first.

1 Put the quantity of chocolate you need in a microwavable bowl. The chocolate should either be in pellet form or chopped into small pieces. Microwave at low power for 30 seconds, then stir it. Stirring is vital even though it appears that nothing has happened.

2 Repeat this process (melt for 30 seconds, then stir vigorously).

3 Repeat again until all the chocolate is melted. At this point the chocolate is tempered. The chocolate should not be hot. If you accidentally go past the 'point of temper', you can pull the chocolate back by simply adding pellets of chocolate one at a time and stirring until they no longer melt into the chocolate (as in the seeding method, opposite).

Making a ganache

There is a great deal written about ganaches and truffles, how exactly they should be made and all the 'rules' regarding them, but for the amateur chocolatier most of this is irrelevant. Ganaches and truffles are essentially the same thing – a chocolate emulsion – presented differently and are really quite simple to make. It is widely thought that an emulsion has to be of cream and chocolate but you can, in fact, have both water and butter ganaches. A water ganache sounds all wrong at first, as chocolate and water are known not to go together, but in fact cream is largely water. A water ganache produces an excellent dairy-free treat for chocolate lovers. You can also replace part or all of the water with alcohol, if you wish. Butter ganache is very smooth and particularly easy to pipe.

Basic recipe

The basic recipe and method for ganaches or truffles remains constant for all but butter ganaches. To produce a selection of flavoured chocolates you can just make up a basic ganache, divide it into parts and flavour each part differently. The proportion of chocolate to liquid should be approximately 2:1 but if you require a softer ganache this can be reduced down as far as 1:1.

1 Measure out 1 part liquid or butter to two parts chocolate, either in pellet form or chopped into small pieces. Place the chocolate in a bowl.

2 If using cream, bring it to the boil first to kill any bacteria and allow the liquid to cool slightly. If using water (or water and alcohol) or butter, heat to hand-hot temperature. Add the warm liquid to the chocolate.

A LIGHTER GANACHE

If you require a ganache that is light in texture you can whip it at this point. This will also increase the volume of the ganache by up to 50 percent. The mixture should be stirred again before use.

Common problems

Very occasionally something goes wrong. The most common problem is that the mix curdles. One reason for this could be that the proportion of chocolate to liquid is out or the temperature of the liquid is too high. Whatever the reason the important thing to know is how to rescue it. Do not throw it away and start again – add a very small amount of boiling water and stir furiously (better still, blitz the mix in a blender). This will nearly always redeem your ganache.

3 Stir well until all the chocolate has been incorporated, then allow the ganache to stand for a while until cool. This will produce a smooth ganache with an extended shelf-life.

Which chocolate works best?

Quite often people will say they only like milk or plain chocolate without actually considering which flavours naturally marry with different chocolates. When you are putting a chocolate together you want the outer chocolate and the inner ganache to work in harmony with each other, neither one overpowering the other. Plain chocolate has the strongest taste of the three types, so needs to be paired with a robust filling. On the other hand, although white chocolate has a less powerful taste, it is much sweeter, which again can clash with a filling.

Some flavours seem to work with all three types of chocolate. These include coffee, orange, pistachio and rum. Flavours like vanilla and banana work well with plain and milk chocolate but are too sweet for white chocolate. Herbs and spices often work better with milk or white chocolate, as plain chocolate can overpower the delicate flavours. The exceptions to this are flavours such as mint and ginger, which are strong in their own right, and also rose and violet, which are heavily perfumed. Cardamom suits white chocolate, while cinnamon, cloves, nutmeg, thyme and rosemary all go well with milk. Saffron is happy with milk or white.

When it comes to alcohol, most spirits work best with plain chocolate. Champagne is quite interesting, as it depends a little on what exactly it is made with (see page 68) but it tends not to suit milk chocolate.

The choice of chocolate is actually far more complex than simply white, milk and plain. If you use single-origin chocolates, you can really go to town on matching up flavours. Single-origin is a concept perhaps more familiar from the worlds of wine and coffee.

Where chocolate is concerned, single-origin denotes a chocolate made with beans sourced from one place, whether that be a particular region or even one specific farm. Single-origin chocolate tends to have very distinct flavours and characteristics, which are influenced by soil and weather conditions and by crops that are grown nearby. Blends of two or more single-origin chocolates will add further scope to the taste options available.

Spices, fruits and other flavourings

This section is really just inspiration for experimentation – the list of suggestions below is not exhaustive. Do remember fresh spices and herbs may be contaminated with pesticides or other non-organic agricultural by-products so it is best to cook them. Also the motto 'less is more' applies here – you require your ingredients to blend nicely not to have overpowering flavours. It is also worth noting that some spices are a little poisonous in large quantities.

HERBS AND LEAVES
Basil – never cook – chop up the leaves and add to the cream at the last minute.
Dill – use the flowers and the seeds. Tastes a bit like fennel with a subtle aniseed flavour.
Green tea – varies enormously. Tea has undergone minimum fermentation and contains antioxidants and caffeine.
Mint – refreshing, strong flavour, good for digestion.

SPICES
Star anise – spicy, only use a little as it can be overpowering.
Cardamom – sweet and spicy.
Cinnamon – warm and spicy with sweet undertones.
Cumin – a bit like anise but more gentle.
Ginger – sharp, sweet and pungent, can boost appetite; thought to be an aphrodisiac.
Lemongrass – mild spicy lemon flavour; can be replaced with lemon zest.

Liquorice – contains a sweetener much stronger than sugar which increases blood pressure.
Saffron – the real thing is expensive but has a lovely aromatic, spicy taste; beware of imitations that just add colour.

OILS
Bergamot – citrusy, fresh.
Jasmine – warm, sweet aromatic essential oil with musk undertones.

FRUITS AND BERRIES
Coconut – grated and dried it is called copra.
Elderberries – must be cooked to remove mildly poisonous bits.
Juniper berries – initial sweet taste but then spicy and tart.
Mango – difficult to use with dairy products such as cream, as it has an enzyme which breaks down proteins . Blanch before using to destroy the enzyme.
Passion fruit – fresh and sour.

Making chocolates

One side of your finished chocolate (this will be the bottom) needs to have a base, which can be made of solid chocolate or something like marzipan. Having a base is very important; it prevents the filling sticking to the dipping fork and possibly being destroyed. It also helps to ensure the chocolate is totally sealed and protected from bacteria. The exception to this is truffles, where you are enrobing by hand and therefore physically covering the entire truffle (see pages 30–31). A chocolate base can be made in two ways.

1 To make a chocolate from a solid filling, such as marzipan or fruit paste (see pages 38–39), place a block of the filling on a sheet of plastic wrap, spread a thin layer of tempered chocolate over the filling and leave until touch dry.

Spreading a base onto a filling

2 Flip the block of filling over and peel off the plastic wrap.

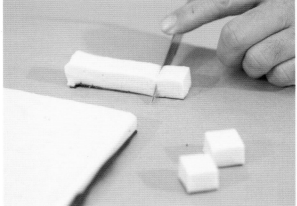

3 Cut the block into the shape and size of chocolate you require. The thin layer of chocolate forms the base. Your chocolates are now ready for dipping (see pages 28–29).

Piping onto a base

1 For softer fillings, such as ganache (see pages 22–23), spread a thin layer of tempered chocolate onto some baking parchment and leave until touch dry.

2 Use pastry cutters to cut out bases from the tempered chocolate to the sizes and shapes you want your finished chocolates to be. Leave the bases to set.

3 Spoon your prepared ganache filling into a large pastry bag fitted with a with a nozzle slightly smaller than your base. To pipe the ganache onto a base, hold the nozzle in the centre of the base and squeeze. Raise the nozzle slightly as the mound of ganache grows, then tilt it to the side. Stop squeezing and 'scrape' the nozzle against the side of the base to release the ganache. Your chocolates are now ready for dipping (see pages 28–29).

Spreading a base onto a soft filling

This method can also be used for soft fillings such as ganache (see pages 22–23), which should be spread into a square or rectangular tin lined with plastic wrap or baking parchment, spread with a thin layer of tempered chocolate, left to dry and then turned out before cutting.

Dipping chocolates

Dipping chocolates or enrobing them has numerous advantages. It makes chocolates look attractive (only rarely is the filling worth looking at, for example the Neapolitan chocolates on page 84), makes them easier to handle (fillings tend to melt much more quickly than the outsides), and it seals the chocolate. Sealing the chocolate is very important if it is to be kept for some time, as the outer case prevents air reaching the more fragile filling, thus increasing the length of time the chocolate remains fresh. When dipping, it is best to use a dipping fork.

These are available at confectionary equipment shops and are purpose-built for the task. The main advantage of the dipping fork is that it has thin tines, which allow the chocolate to slip off easily without leaving any marks. You can use an ordinary fork, however. Before you start, ensure that the chocolates are set and at room temperature. Make sure the dipping fork is at room temperature too – if the fork is extremely cold the chocolate will not slide off easily. If the fork is too warm it will knock the chocolate off temper.

1 In a bowl, temper enough good-quality chocolate to lower the chocolates into so that they are totally covered. Lower a chocolate into the bowl on a dipping fork. Use the fork to flick tempered chocolate over the chocolate until covered. The recipes in this book give approximate quantities of chocolate for dipping, as the amount you use will depend on your skill.

Removing the 'feet'

The final stage of dipping your chocolates requires you to remove any 'feet' on the chocolate. These are the little bits of chocolate around the base where it hasn't set quite neatly. Remove these carefully with a sharp knife.

2 Slide the dipping fork under the base of the chocolate and lift out carefully. Rest the fork on the edge of the bowl and gently tap the excess chocolate off the dipped chocolate.

3 Gently slide the chocolate towards the edge of the bowl, scraping off excess before sliding the chocolate off the dipping fork onto greaseproof paper. You can decorate your chocolates at this point (see pages 46–55) while the wet chocolate acts as glue, or leave to set at room temperature. Refrigeration may cause them to sweat and will adversely affect the appearance and taste. When your chocolates are finished, remember to cut off the 'feet' (see above).

Dipping truffles

The better way to dip truffles is literally by hand. Basically all you are doing is covering your fingers with tempered chocolate and rolling the truffle around until it is coated. Sometimes a second coat is required after the first has set. It can be fun and it adds a second layer of taste, if you use a different chocolate in the second dipping. If using different chocolates make sure the first coat is totally dry before rolling in the second.

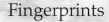

Fingerprints

To avoid leaving fingerprints when handling your chocolates, you can use gloves. It would be a shame to spoil the finish on your chocolates at this final stage.

1 In a bowl, temper good-quality chocolate of your choice. Dip the three middle fingers of each hand in the tempered chocolate and pick up a truffle. Roll the truffle in your fingers – not in your palm, as this will be too warm and will melt the truffle – until the truffle is well coated. You may need to dip your fingers more than once to cover one truffle.

2 The truffles can then be left to dry before rolling again in chocolate, or can be rolled in chopped nuts, crushed amaretti biscuits, coconut, cocoa powder, icing sugar or any other coating you might like.

Moulding chocolates

It is not always ideal to dip your chocolates. Sometimes, for example, the centre may be very soft or liquid and this would make dipping virtually impossible. Also, unless you are exceptionally talented, you are limited in what shapes and patterns you can achieve using a dipping technique. The solution to these issues is to use moulds. Although chocolatiers have lots of professional chocolate moulds, there are many inexpensive ways to mould chocolate at home.

Mould essentials

Moulds must not be porous, must be shiny and must have some level of flexibility. Bearing these three criteria in mind, many household items make suitable moulds:

ICE CUBE TRAYS These are inexpensive, relatively easy to use and come in lots of different shapes and sizes.

JELLY MOULDS Many jelly moulds are too large but it is possible to find small ones if you look around. You can use the large ones to make chocolate figures.

CANAPÉ MOULDS Metal moulds can be very difficult to use as their lack of flexibility makes it tricky to get the chocolate to release. Also, because they aren't transparent, you can't check the mould is totally covered. You can get some made from polycarbonate (plastic) and these work well.

MOULDS FROM CHILDREN'S ACTIVITY KITS Designed for soap, plaster and so on, these can also be used. Wash and dry thoroughly before use.

PLASTIC SEASONAL CONTAINERS For example, the inside of a chocolate advent calendar or Easter egg packaging.

The list really is endless. Just use your imagination and take care that what you are using is suitable for food.

1 Clean and polish your mould so that your chocolates will release easily when set.

2 Using tempered chocolate (see pages 18–21) and a clean finger, paint a thin layer of chocolate over all of the inside of the mould. This ensures that the chocolate goes into any crevices and means you don't have holes in the finished chocolates. Leave to set.

3 Spoon tempered chocolate into the mould until each section is full (it is often easier to do this with half the mould at a time). Bang the mould down firmly on a surface three times – you'll see air bubbles rise to the top.

4 Tip the chocolate out of the mould, banging on the side of the mould as you do, so that all the excess chocolate is removed. This gives a second coating of chocolate. Although you want to have a good covering of chocolate, it should also be thin and crisp. Carefully remove any excess chocolate on the top of the mould using either a palette knife or your finger to make filling easier.

5 Turn the moulds upside down onto greaseproof paper to ensure any excess chocolate comes away as it sets. When the chocolate is totally set, use a piping bag to fill the moulds with your chosen ganache. The ganache needs to be fairly soft in order to pipe it but be careful not to make the mistake of using hot ganache as this could knock your chocolate off temper. Fill each section to just below the top to allow space for the base, then leave to set.

6 Using a palette knife, spread tempered chocolate onto the fully set ganache, removing any excess. This will form the base of the chocolate.

Presentation

Once you've made your delicious and beautiful chocolates, either by dipping or moulding, then you will want to make the effort to present them well, especially if you plan to give them as a gift. Have a look at the chapter on presentation (pages 44–61) for some ideas.

7 When set, turn the chocolates out of the mould by tapping or very gently twisting the mould, if necessary. Using a sharp knife, cut away any unsightly 'feet' from the chocolates (see page 29).

Crystallizing fruit

You will be amazed at how different homemade crystallized peel tastes to its shop-bought alternative. It is so juicy! The peel from citrus and other fruits has numerous uses. It can be simply dipped in chocolate for a zingy and indulgent treat, it can be used as a decoration or as part of a chocolate filling. The process does take about a week to make good crystallized peel but the method involved is not complicated. For ideas on how to use crystallized fruit peel as decoration on your chocolates, see page 48.

Crystallized orange or grapefruit peel

INGREDIENTS

6 large oranges or grapefruit, peeled (discard the flesh)

Water

Approx 1.2 litres (2 pints) simple syrup

10–11 tablespoons sugar

1 Place the peel into a saucepan of water. Bring to the boil and simmer until the peel is soft – this is essential, as otherwise the peel will become hard when crystallized.

2 Drain the peel and discard the water. Make a simple sugar solution (1 part water to 1 part sugar), enough to cover the peel. Pour over the drained peel and bring to the boil. Turn off the heat, cover and leave to cool for 4–6 hours or overnight. When completely cool, add 1 1/2 tablespoons sugar and bring to the boil before covering and cooling once more. Repeat this system of adding sugar and boiling for seven consecutive days.

Crystallized ginger

It is the flesh of ginger that is crystallized, not the peel. Ginger is very tough, so it will need to be boiled for much longer until it is soft. A lot of the flavour goes into the water so the water is not thrown away; instead sugar is added to it to create a simple syrup.

Crystallized pineapple

Again, it is the flesh that is crystallized. It doesn't require a long boil and the water can be reused, as for ginger. You can cheat by using good quality tinned pineapple.

3 After seven days, the peel should be translucent and the liquid will be the consistency of double cream. If not quite there, keep adding sugar, boiling and cooling until it is.

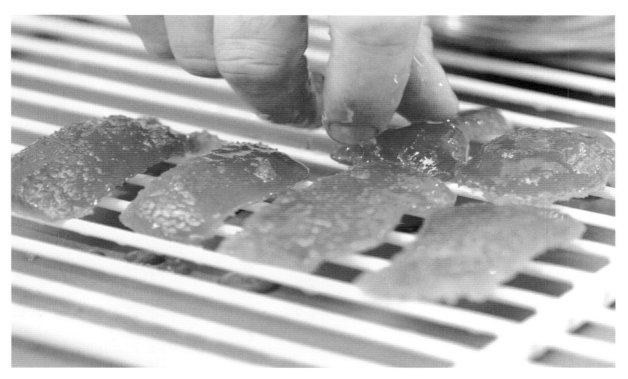

4 Drain the the liquid away (keep it in a sealed jar and use it as a flavoured syrup). Lay the fruit strips across a rack and allow to drain and dry fully. Store in an airtight container.

Fruit paste

Fruit pastes are an ancient confectionery and were documented as far back as the Middle Ages. Known by their French name, *pâtes de fruits,* they were made primarily as a way of preserving fruit. A fruit paste is effectively a very heavily thickened jam that can be cut or sliced. The paste can then be eaten as it is or covered in sugar or used in chocolates (see the page opposite for how to dip fruit pastes).

The recipes using fruit paste in this book employ it as a layer within a chocolate. Fruit pastes are ideal for this – they can be spread onto a lightly greased tray or a non-stick silicone mat and left to set. The set paste is then used as a layer with caramels, pralines and so on. The fruit paste has a totally different texture to other chocolate fillings and is colourful, producing an attractive sight when the chocolate is cut or bitten into.

The fruits set because of the presence of pectin, which is a gummy substance released when most fruits are boiled. The pectin only works as a gum in the presence of acid and sugar. The acid comes naturally from the fruit but fruits vary in their acidity and pectin content. Fruits with high pectin content include apples, apricots, blackcurrants, lemons, cranberries, gooseberries, prunes, oranges and blackberries. If you are making a fruit paste from one of these then you can substantially reduce the quantity of pectin added. Quite often some apricot or apple purée is added to pastes to naturally increase the pectin levels of low-pectin fruits. Alternatively, pectin can be bought as a powder. A little tartaric acid is added to enhance the fruit flavours.

Fruit pastes are really vibrant in colour. Once set you can spread over a ganache, a caramel or a different fruit paste. You can add crunchy pieces, such as nuts, cocoa nibs and popping candy.

Raspberry fruit paste

INGREDIENTS

15 g (1/2 oz) pectin in powder form

300 g (10 oz) sugar

300 g (10 oz) raspberry pulp (heat the raspberries in a pan with a tiny amount of water, then squash with a spoon or fork)

Pinch of tartaric acid dissolved in a little water

Testing the temperature

Put a couple of saucers into the freezer. When you think the fruit mixture is at the correct temperature, take out a frozen saucer and put a little of the mix onto it carefully (it will be very, very hot!). If the mixture is at the right temperature you will be able to push it about like jelly. As you push it, it will wrinkle.

1 Tip the pectin into a large heavy-based pan and mix in a little of the sugar. This prevents the pectin from clotting.

2 Add the raspberry pulp, mix together and bring to the boil. Heat until you reach a temperature of 108°C (226°F). This is easiest to measure using a digital thermometer. Or use the traditional but less accurate method (see opposite). When correct temperature is reached, add the tartaric mixture and stir well.

3 Place a non-stick silicone mat inside a 20 x 20 cm (8 x 8 in) tin with sides over 1.5 cm (½ in) deep. Or line with plastic wrap. Pour fruit mixture into the tin so that it is about 1.5 cm (½ in) deep and leave to set.

4 When set, use as a filling for a chocolate or simply cut into pieces and coat in granulated sugar for an excellent gift or after-dinner treat.

Dipping strawberries

Simply perfect! Chocolate strawberries have only two ingredients – chocolate and strawberries. What could be simpler? They taste divine and bring to mind lazy summer days.

The weights in this recipe are very approximate as they depend on the size of the strawberries but I've included them to give some guidelines. It is essential that you only use perfect, fresh fruit. If the strawberries are at all soft then the chocolate won't adhere to them and you'll end up with a rather unpleasant oozing mess. Which chocolate you use is entirely down to taste. Some people prefer a rich dark chocolate to complement the sweetness of the fruit, others the creamy white chocolate reminding them of strawberries and cream.

For both of the following recipes, start by putting the strawberries in the fridge while you temper your chocolate (see pages 18–21). Cooling the fruit down is a little bit of a cheat, as it means that the chocolate will still work even if it isn't 100 percent tempered. I always temper more chocolate than I need, since there is always some waste as the chocolate remaining in the bowl becomes too shallow to dip the strawberries into. Use a narrow container to avoid waste.

Double dipping

These look and taste so good. Dip approximately two-thirds of each strawberry in tempered plain chocolate and leave to dry. Once dry, dip the tips of the fruit into tempered white chocolate and leave to dry. This results in a stunning look of green stalk, red fruit, dark and finally white chocolate.

Chocolate strawberries

INGREDIENTS

500 g (1 lb) strawberries

50 g (1¾ oz) chocolate, tempered

1 Remove the strawberries from the fridge and gently pat with kitchen paper to remove any dampness. Hold the fruit by the stem and half dip into the chocolate. Allow the excess chocolate to fall back into the bowl, gently spinning the strawberry while you do this to encourage more of the excess to fall into the bowl. Place the strawberry on greaseproof paper or baking parchment to dry.

Black tie strawberries

These strawberries are so simple to make and are quite a striking and fun treat to serve at the end of a dinner party.

INGREDIENTS

500 g (1 lb) strawberries

50 g (1¾ oz) white chocolate, tempered

50 g (1¾ oz) dark chocolate

1 Follow the instructions for making chocolate strawberries, opposite, using white chocolate. While the white chocolate is drying, temper the dark chocolate, then holding a strawberry at a diagonal, dip a third into the dark chocolate and shake very gently, allowing the excess to fall into the bowl. Do not spin the strawberry.

2 Hold the same strawberry at the opposite angle and dip another third into the dark chocolate to create a V-shape to resemble the lapels of a dinner jacket. Place the strawberry V-shape up on greaseproof paper or baking parchment to dry.

3 Continue dipping all the strawberries. When dry, make a piping bag (see pages 42–43) and fill with the remaining dark chocolate from the bowl. Pipe chocolate bow ties onto the white chocolate and leave to dry.

Making a piping bag

One essential weapon in anyone's chocolate armoury is knowing how to make a piping bag. Admittedly, you can buy ready-made piping bags but they are always big, and while this makes them ideal for piping ganache, they are no use at all for any delicate work, particularly adding those extra bits of detail that will make your chocolates look stunning.

Learning to make a piping bag is a bit like learning to ride a bike – it can seem impossible at first but once you've learned how, you never forget.

When using a piping bag remember never to overfill it – about a third full is sensible. Once you've filled the bag, roll down the top. Apply a little pressure at this fold – you may find that the chocolate comes out of the tip or it may be necessary to make a very small cut across the tip. You can vary the size of the hole to give the thickness of flow required.

Never press down in the centre of the bag, always apply pressure at the top or you'll force the chocolate out of the top of the bag, resulting in a horrible mess. Keep turning down the top of the bag in the same way you would turn down a tube of toothpaste.

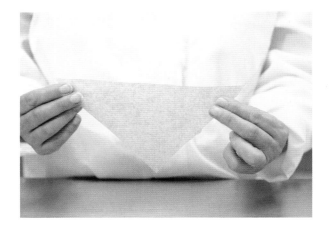

1 Cut a piece of greaseproof paper or baking parchment approximately 10 cm (4 in) square. Obviously the size is determined by what you are doing but this is quite an easy size to learn on. Cut straight across the diagonal of the square to give two right-angled triangles

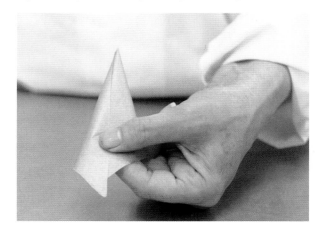

4 Continue pulling the same point all the way across the front and then round the back until that point meets up at the front with the other two points, giving you a cone.

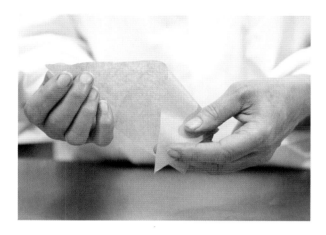

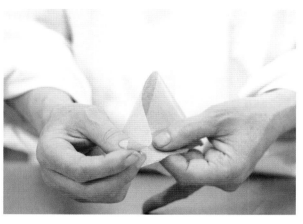

2 Hold the triangle so that the longest side is at the top. Put two fingers of your left hand in the centre of the triangle for support and, using the thumb of the same hand, bring down the left point of the triangle until it meets up with the bottom point of the triangle.

3 Using your right hand, take the right point of the triangle down past the point where the other two points meet.

5 Without letting go, tilt the tip of the cone towards you and turn over the points twice in order to hold your piping bag securely.

6 You now have your bag. Don't worry if you haven't succeeded – undo what you've done and try again. It will become easy with practice.

Presentation

Delicious-looking chocolates, presented beautifully, make fantastic gifts and will have mouths salivating. Even simple chocolates will benefit from pretty decoration and stylish packaging.

Decorating chocolates

You can add decoration to your chocolates in a number of ways, including simply adding decoration to the top and creating textured effects using different materials. All the methods are fairly simple and can create stunning results.

The most important factor to consider is that the chocolates are made to the best possible standard.

Remember to cut off the 'feet' – the little bits of chocolate sticking out at the base of the chocolate (see page 29) to tidy up the edges. Handle your chocolates carefully, preferably with latex gloves (or similar), so that you don't get fingerprints on the finished article. As well as decorating individual chocolates, you can decorate a plate of them to serve.

Dipping fork decoration

Try touching a dipping fork to the top of the chocolate while it is still wet, then carefully lift it off. This will leave three ridges – don't worry if it smudges at first, you will get it right with practice. Another option is to turn the fork on its side to make one ridge.

Shiny chocolate

There is a chocolate called *Palet d'or*, famous for its very shiny surface. This is a subtle, elegant way to make your chocolates look different and it is easy to achieve, particularly on plain chocolate. As soon as you dip your chocolate, press a piece of shiny foil onto its top. For maximum shine wait ten hours before peeling it off again but you will achieve a degree of shine in half an hour.

Nuts

Whole nuts, roasted nuts, chopped nuts, powdered nuts – in fact, all forms of nuts can be used to decorate your chocolates. Place any whole, chopped or flaked nuts on top of just-dipped chocolates so they stick as the chocolate sets.

Crystallized fruit peel and grated zest

For instructions on how to crystallize fruit peel, see pages 36–37. To use it as a decoration simply cut thin strips or circles and place onto a chocolate while it is still damp. Grated zest is a very simple ornament for a fruity chocolate and is particularly nice if crystallized. You can't crystallize zest in the same way you would crystallize fruit, as it is too fine and would lose all its taste.

1 Simply grate the zest of a citrus fruit of your choice, then dip it into a simple sugar syrup, made by boiling 1 part sugar in 1 part water until the sugar has dissolved.

2 Leave the dipped zest to dry, then place on top of just-dipped chocolates so the peel sticks as the chocolate sets.

Crystallized flowers

Rose petals, violets or other edible flowers make beautiful decorations. They need to be crystallized before use but as they are very fragile, they have to be crystallized using egg white, not a sugar syrup.

Although very little egg is used, there are some potential health risks when using raw egg. If this is of concern, you can use reconstituted egg white instead of fresh.

1 Dry petals or whole flowers very slowly in a relatively low oven.

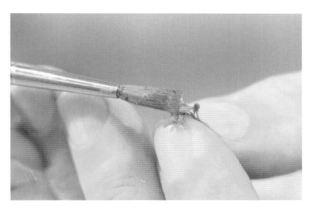

2 Coat the petals or flowers in egg white using a soft, clean paintbrush.

3 Very gently roll the egg white-coated petals or flowers in caster sugar.

4 Immediately place on top of a dipped chocolate. The egg white will absorb the sugar and dry out, leaving the petal or flower crystallized.

Transfer sheets

These are sheets of acetate on which a pattern has been painted using colourings dissolved in cocoa butter. When tempered chocolate is spread onto a sheet and sets, it pulls away, taking the pattern with it. To colour a group of just-dipped chocolates, invert a sheet on top of them.

Textured papers

A different type of acetate sheet is one with a textured surface. If you place a textured sheet on top of a chocolate or spread chocolate onto it, and leave it to set, the textured imprint is transferred onto the chocolate. Experiment with bubble wrap or textured plastics found in DIY stores.

1 Spread some tempered chocolate onto a patterned transfer sheet (or invert the sheet on top of a group of just-dipped chocolates) and leave the chocolate to set.

1 Spread some tempered chocolate onto a piece of textured plastic (or invert a sheet on top of a group of just-dipped chocolates) and leave the chocolate to set.

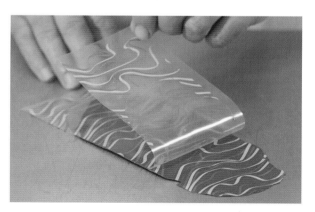

2 When set, carefully peel back the sheet. Cut out shapes to serve as thins or follow the instructions on pages 122–123.

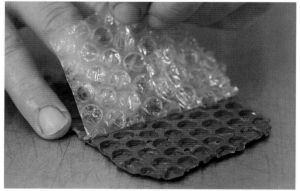

2 When set, carefully peel back the plastic from the chocolate. Cut out shapes to serve.

Piped detail

To pipe delicate shapes and patterns with chocolate you will need to make your own piping bag, as bought bags are generally too big for the task. For instructions on how to make a piping bag see pages 42–43. It is worth practising your piping skills on paper until you feel confident.

1 Temper a small amount of chocolate (see pages 18–21) and spoon it into a homemade piping bag (see pages 42–43).

2 Wind down the bag from the open end and snip the very tip off the bag.

3 The simplest type of detail is achieved by moving quickly over the chocolates, piping thin parallel lines. You could have an interesting pattern or just something random. Alternatively, piping can indicate flavour, for example a stylized 'M' piped on a mint chocolate. Or you could draw a shape that indicates the flavour, for example, an outline of a fig. If your chocolates are for a special occasion, such as a birthday, engagement or wedding then try piping on names, initials or numbers. The personal touch can make a huge difference to the end result.

Chocolate leaves

These are great fun for adults and children to make and they are superb decorations for chocolates or desserts. Real leaves are used so please make sure they are edible. Small leaves can be fixed to individual chocolates and larger leaves can be mixed in with chocolates on a serving plate. This looks particularly attractive if you vary the colours of the leaves. You could, for example, have a stunning array of coloured and white-chocolate autumn leaves.

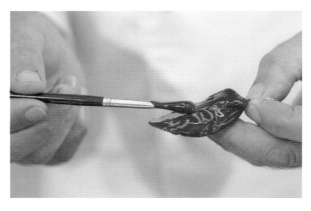

1 Using a soft, clean paintbrush, spread a layer of tempered chocolate (see pages 18–21) on the underside of a clean, fresh, dry leaf. The layer should be thick enough to allow it to come away from the leaf without cracking when dry. Using the underside of the leaf will produce clearer veins on your chocolate leaf.

2 Leave to set for about 20 minutes, then gently peel away the real leaf from the chocolate shape.

3 The finished chocolate leaf should have all the markings of the real leaf and look really quite stunning.

Curls, flakes and cigarillos

The methods of making these are very similar – in fact, until you are quite practised, you will often end up with flakes regardless. You will need a metal scraper of the kind sold in DIY stores. It should be quite flexible and as wide as the rolls you are trying to make.

1 Temper some chocolate (see pages 18–21). Using a palette knife, spread the chocolate onto a sealed marble or granite surface or large marble tile. Leave to set until touch dry.

2 Hold a metal scraper at a roughly 45°-angle at the edge of the chocolate and push it along the chocolate. For flakes, scrape in quick, short motions at the set chocolate.

3 For curls, scrape more slowly so that the chocolate rolls in on itself. It may need a helping finger to encourage it to roll.

4 For cigarillos, the hardest technique of the three, cut two straight edges so the chocolate is the exact width you need. Push your scraper firmly and slowly at a 45°-angle, encouraging the chocolate to curl into a tight cigarillo as you go.

Chocolate grids

These are surprisingly easy to make but look very professional. The grids can be of any size and can be put over a group of chocolates displayed on a plate, used to top a presentation box (see page 57) or made into fan shapes to decorate the tops of individual chocolates. You could try combining lines of different coloured chocolates and vary the shape of your lines.

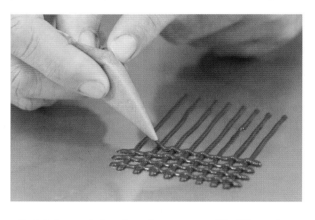

1 Make a piping bag (see pages 42–43) and fill it with tempered chocolate (see pages 18–21). On a piece of plastic wrap or acetate, pipe parallel lines close to each other and then pipe lines at right angles to these to form a grid.

2 Leave the grid to set, then either break it or cut it with a warm knife into pieces of the size you want.

3 Use small pieces to decorate individual chocolates or lay larger grids across a group of chocolates on a plate to serve.

Grid shapes

Fun shapes can be created by drawing a template on paper and tracing it onto plastic wrap or acetate using piped chocolate. Hold the template and acetate together with blobs of chocolate.

Colouring chocolate

You can colour white chocolate using either powder or oil-based paste colours. Do not use liquid colours as they will cause the chocolate to seize.

1 Make a piping bag (see pages 42–43) and fill with tempered chocolate (see pages 18–21). Place the template beneath the cellophane or acetate and pipe chocolate around the outline.

1 Melt the quantity of white chocolate you wish to colour (see page 18). Using a spoon, add a little powdered colouring to the chocolate.

2 Fill in the shape with a grid, piping first parallel lines and then another set of parallel lines at right angles to those. If you like, the outline can be a different coloured chocolate to the grid that fills it.

2 Mix thoroughly, adding colouring little by little and mixing each time until you have the colour and intensity you want.

Packaging

Your chocolates now look great but putting in an extra bit of effort to create beautiful packaging will turn them into the ultimate gift or table centrepiece. Edible chocolate packaging is great fun and particularly suitable for presenting chocolates at the table. If you are planning to give your chocolates as a gift, however, conventional, non-edible packaging makes more sense.

Chocolate box

Draw and cut out templates for the base and each side of your box in card or plastic. You can also cut a lid, if you wish (or use a grid – see page 54 for instructions on making grids). Consider how many chocolates you want to fit inside the box so you know how deep to make the sides and how large the base needs to be.

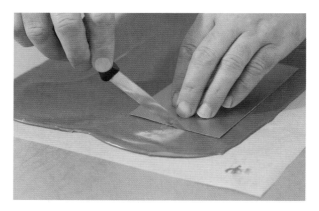

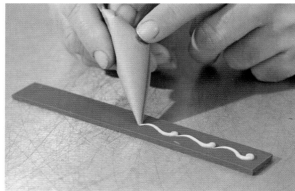

1 Temper some chocolate (see pages 18–21). As a guide, for about 15 chocolates you will need a box approximately 15 x 9 x 2.5 cm (6 x 3¹/₂ x 1 in) this box will require about 250 g (9 oz) chocolate. Using a palette knife, spread tempered chocolate onto a marble slab or baking parchment so it is about 50 mm (¹/₅ in) thick. Leave until touch dry, then using your templates, cut out all four sides and the base and lid (if using) for your box.

2 Leave the sides to set completely. While you have your box in pieces and more importantly flat, you can decorate it. Fill homemade piping bags (see pages 42–43) with different coloured chocolates (see page 55). These can then be used to write messages or to draw patterns on your box. Do consider whether you are writing on the inside or the outside.

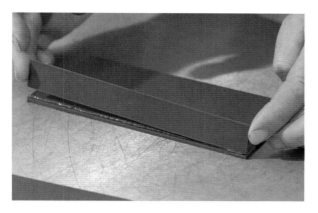

3 Leave your decoration to set and dry completely. The box now needs to be put together. Using a piping bag of tempered chocolate, pipe a thin line of chocolate along one side of the base (you can use a contrasting type of chocolate but this is more difficult as any slips are very obvious). Stick the appropriate side onto it and hold or support it in place until the piece starts to set.

4 Next, pipe a line of chocolate along the adjacent side of the base. Take your next side and pipe chocolate along the vertical edge, which will join with the side already fixed. Now put this piece in place. Keep going until all the sides are attached, remembering that you can support the edges while they set.

5 To attach a lid, balance it so it is open and stick it firmly in place with tempered chocolate. You may need to pipe an additional line of chocolate along the join when the lid is in place to give added strength. An alternative to a lid is to use a grid (see page 54). A grid is considerably lighter than a solid lid and is less likely to collapse. If you have not already decorated your box, you can do so now. You could use coloured sweets – just stick them in place using tempered chocolate as glue.

Chocolate platter

This next method allows you to create a malleable sheet of chocolate that can be shaped or cut into an interesting platter on which to display your chocolates. It can also be used as a neat, flat covering for a cake. You will need a sealed marble or granite tile or slab. When the melted chocolate hits the cold slab, it is shocked by the dramatic change in temperature and changes in form. You have to work very quickly with the resulting sheet, as once it sets it will no longer be malleable.

1 Put a sealed marble tile in the freezer for at least 3 hours. Melt some chocolate (this does not need to be tempered). Remove the tile from the freezer and quickly spread a thin layer of chocolate over it using a pallete knife.

2 The chocolate changes in form, solidifying quickly and will lift off the slab as a continuous flat sheet.

3 While the chocolate is still slightly maleable, very quickly cut or manipulate the sheet into a shape of your choice.

4 Use the platter to serve or display your chocolates. It makes an excellent centrepiece when serving coffee after a meal.

Chocolate container

This is quite a fun way to create a basket or container in which to display your chocolates.

It is worth experimenting with different patterns and shapes but start with something simple.

1 Blow up a balloon until it is well but not completely inflated. Do not tie the balloon to seal it, but fasten it closed with a bulldog clip. Find a way to hold the balloon still (your knees or a friend may be useful).

2 Temper some chocolate (see pages 18–21) and fill a piping bag (see pages 42–43) with it. Pipe a pattern over an area the size of the container you require. Keep the gaps between the lines small so the container is stable.

3 When the chocolate is set it will start to pull away from the balloon. When this happens, very carefully release the bulldog clip to let small amounts of air out of the balloon at a time. Keep going until you can lift the balloon out, leaving behind your chocolate container.

4 You now have a beautiful but fragile container for your chocolates and you can eat it once the chocolates are gone.

Table favours

To make simple but stunning table favours, cut a square of cellophane and place a chocolate or truffle in the centre. Gather up all the edges of the square and tie them together a little above the chocolate with some pretty ribbon. Carefully tease out the cellophane ends above the ribbon so that they fan out above the chocolate. Curl the ribbon. Your favour can be balanced on its side to give maximum impact.

Boxes and baskets

Firstly, decide on the shape you want your box to be. Simple cuboid shapes are by far the easiest boxes to make. Consider how many chocolates you want to fit inside the box so you know how deep to make the sides and how large the base. Next, choose some pretty card or personalize plain card with a message, block printing or other design work.

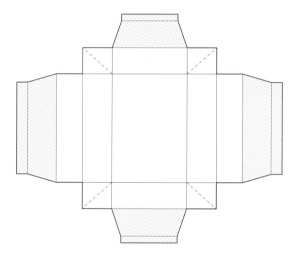

1 Draw a template for your box – this is how it would look if it were flat. The example above is for a simple, shallow, rectangular box. Add flaps to the template (see shaded areas above), which will enable you to fasten the sides of the box together. These can be very simple or you can create an entire inner layer, which is often more attractive and effective, as the coloured or decorated side of the card will be visible on the inside of the box. The larger the flaps, the stronger the box will be.

2 Carefully cut out the template and score along all the fold lines of the box with sharp scissors or a scalpel, using a ruler as a guide if you don't have a particularly steady hand.

3 Fold in the edges of the box along the score lines and secure them as neatly as you can with glue or tape.

4 You can fill the box with chocolates or buy an insert, which will help keep the chocolates in place. If you want to make the box into a basket you can make a handle out of the same card and attach it to opposite sides of the box – do remember it will not be very strong! If you want a lid for your box, make one in the same way you made the box, by starting with a template. The lid will need a slightly larger base than the box so it will fit over the top.

Chocolates

Dipped chocolates

Hand-dipping chocolates does require a little practice. Remember that the finished product can only be as neat as the filling – dipping won't hide misformed chocolates. If a recipe calls for the cream to be boiled, this only needs to be done if the chocolates are being kept for a time. If eaten the same day, the cream only needs to be heated until hot enough to melt the chocolate.

This might sound more like something you'd have with lamb but it makes a lovely chocolate! Lots of different herbs can be used in chocolates – you'll be amazed at the results. If using fresh herbs, make sure they are clean. This recipe uses milk chocolate because herbs, on the whole, have a fairly delicate flavour, which can be over-powered by plain chocolate.

Rosemary and thyme

INGREDIENTS

100 ml (3 1/2 fl oz) double cream

1 1/2 teaspoons water

7 g (1/4 oz) fresh rosemary, finely chopped – check the rosemary is in good condition

1.5 g (pinch) dried thyme

Pinch salt

450 g (16 oz) milk chocolate, chopped or in pellet form

1 Boil the cream with the water and herbs for two minutes, then leave to infuse for 10 minutes. Pass the infusion through a sieve, pressing the herbs firmly with a wooden spoon to squeeze out the flavour, then reheat the infusion but do not boil.

2 Place the salt and 200 g (7 oz) of the milk chocolate in a bowl and pour over the warm infusion. Stir until fully incorporated. If you still have lumps of chocolate, warm the mixture for about 10 seconds in the microwave and stir again. Pour the mixture into a 25 x 25 cm (10 x 10 in) tin lined with plastic wrap or baking parchment.

3 Temper the 250 g (9 oz) milk chocolate for dipping (see pages 18–21) and spread a thin layer over the ganache. Leave to set. When the chocolate is touch dry, cut into oblongs, dipping your knife into water between cuts to prevent sticking. You must shake off the water after you dip the knife to prevent spoiling the chocolate. Leave to set completely.

4 Dip each chocolate into the tempered milk chocolate and mark with a dipping fork before leaving to set. When set, use a sharp knife cut away any 'feet' (see page 29).

The addition of grapefruit to the Champagne ganache produces a really tangy chocolate with an intense burst of flavour. Marc de Champagne compound, which gives a stronger flavour than Champagne itself, is available in some delis and good food halls or can be obtained online.

Grapefruit and Champagne squares

INGREDIENTS

100 ml (3 1/2 fl oz) double cream

250 g (9 oz) Swiss milk chocolate

20 g (3/4 oz) Marc de Champagne compound

Vanilla essence (few drops)

Grapefruit peel, freshly grated

Crystallized grapefruit peel, finely chopped (see pages 36–37)

275 g (9 3/4 oz) Swiss white chocolate, for dipping

For Orange Champagne squares substitute the white chocolate for milk chocolate and add 1 teaspoon orange liqueur to the ganache, then dip in rich dark chocolate.

1 Line a 20 x 20 cm (8 x 8 in) shallow tin with plastic wrap or baking parchment.

2 Warm the cream, add the Swiss milk chocolate to it and stir until smooth. Stir in the Champagne compound and vanilla, then whip the mixture for a few minutes to lighten it, pour into the prepared tin and leave to set.

3 Temper the white chocolate (see pages 18–21) and spread a thin layer over the ganache. When set, turn over so that the thin layer of chocolate now forms the base and cut into 2.5 cm (1 in) squares (makes about 64 pieces).

4 Mix the fresh and crystallized grapefruit peels together and use a little white chocolate to stick some of the peel mixture to the top of each square. Dip in Swiss white chocolate and leave to set. When set, use a sharp knife to cut away any 'feet' (see page 29).

Hawberries give a real tang to the oranges in this chocolate. They are available in delis and health food shops but you can substitute chopped dried cranberries, dried cherries or barberries.

Hawberry and orange delight

INGREDIENTS

120 g (4 oz) dried hawberries

Juice of 6 oranges (the peel can be crystallized, see pages 36–37)

280 ml (9 fl oz) double cream

500 g (1 lb) milk chocolate, chopped or in pellet form

500 g (1 lb) dark chocolate, chopped or in pellet form, for dipping

A few dried hawberries for decoration

1 Line a 750 ml (1 1/4 pint) capacity tin with plastic wrap. In a pan, boil the hawberries in the orange juice until the juice has reduced by half.

2 Boil the cream then allow it to cool slightly. Add the chopped milk chocolate and stir well until it is fully incorporated. If you still have lumps of chocolate, warm the mixture for about 10 seconds in the microwave and stir again.

3 Stir in the juice and hawberries, then pour or spoon the mixture into the prepared tin and leave to set.

4 Temper about a third of the dark chocolate (see pages 18–21) and spread a thin layer over the mixture. Leave to set. When set, turn out onto baking parchment so the chocolate layer is at the bottom. Cut into 1.5 cm (3/4 inch) squares, dipping your knife in water and shaking it between each cut to prevent sticking.

5 Temper the remainder of the dark chocolate and dip each square to fully seal it. Before it has set, decorate each chocolate with a dried hawberry, then leave to set before cutting away any 'feet' from the chocolate (see page 29).

Although it sounds like a savoury chocolate, this is in fact quite sweet. Tomatoes are fruits and become sweet especially when sun-dried. Take care when buying sun-dried tomatoes in olive oil that the product does not contain any herbs, spices or garlic, as this will destroy the taste of your chocolate.

Taste of the Mediterranean

INGREDIENTS

125 ml (4 fl oz) double cream

250 g (9 oz) extra bitter dark chocolate (70% cocoa), chopped or in pellet form

30 g (1 ¼ oz) sun-dried tomatoes in olive oil, finely chopped

275 g (10 oz) plain chocolate, chopped or in pellet form, for dipping

1 Line a 20 x 20 cm (8 x 8 in) shallow tin, with plastic wrap or baking parchment. In a pan, boil the cream, then allow it to cool slightly.

2 Add the chopped plain chocolate and stir well until it is fully incorporated. If you still have lumps of chocolate, warm the mixture for about 10 seconds in the microwave and stir again. Add the finely chopped sun-dried tomatoes, then spoon or pour the ganache into the prepared tin and leave to set.

3 Temper about a third of the dipping chocolate (see pages 18–21) and spread a thin layer over the ganache. Leave to set. When set, turn out onto a sheet of baking parchment, with the chocolate layer at the bottom and cut into diamond shapes approximately 1.5 cm (3/4 in) long, dipping your knife in water and shaking it between each cut to prevent sticking.

4 Temper the remaining dark chocolate for dipping and dip each diamond shape so it is fully sealed, then leave to set before cutting away any 'feet' from the chocolate (see page 29).

Making praline paste requires effort and experience so it is easier and cheaper to buy it ready-made from confectionery suppliers. Roast the hazelnuts yourself – they will taste so much better. Put a single layer of hazelnuts in a pan. Place over a low heat (don't add any oil or water), then simply heat until they go a light brown colour. Stir them and make sure they don't burn.

Praline squares

INGREDIENTS

100 ml (3 1/2 fl oz) double cream

175 g (6 oz) milk chocolate, chopped or in pellet form

25 g (1 oz) praline paste

200 g (7 oz) milk chocolate, chopped or in pellet form, for dipping

25 g (1 oz) hazelnuts, roasted and chopped, for decoration

For Praline marzipan squares cut circles of thinly rolled-out marzipan. Pipe the ganache onto the marzipan bases. Leave to set and dip.

For Pistachio praline squares fold 2 tbsp finely chopped pistachios into the ganache instead of finely chopped hazelnuts.

1 Line a 20 x 20 cm (8 x 8 in) shallow tin with plastic wrap or baking parchment. Bring the cream to the boil in a pan and allow it to cool slightly.

2 Add 175 g (6 oz) milk chocolate and stir until all the chocolate is incorporated. If you still have lumps of chocolate, warm the mixture for about 10 seconds in the microwave and stir again. Add the praline paste and stir. Spread into the prepared tin.

3 Temper 200 g (7 oz) milk chocolate for dipping and spread a thin layer over the ganache. Leave to set. When touch dry, cut into squares, dipping your knife in water and shaking it between each cut to prevent sticking. Leave to set completely.

4 When set, dip each chocolate in the remaining tempered milk chocolate so it is fully sealed. Scatter some of the hazelnuts on each chocolate, then leave to set before cutting away any 'feet' from the chocolate (see page 29).

The crisp, rich, slightly bitter dark chocolate contrasts beautifully with the soft, tangy apricot centre. Although this recipe only uses a third of the apricot paste, it is easier to make the whole amount, cut the excess into cubes, dredge in sugar and keep in an airtight container. It makes a yummy fruity treat for children and adults alike.

Apricot pavé

INGREDIENTS

200 g (7 oz) apricot paste
 (see pages 38–39)

150 g (5 oz) dark chocolate, chopped
 or in pellet form, for dipping

For Brandy-soaked apricot pavé soak some chopped, dried apricots in brandy overnight and sprinkle these on top of the paste while it is still liquid. When set and before any 'feet' have been removed, dip the corner of each chocolate into tempered white chocolate. Before this sets, place a small piece of dried apricot on each corner.

1 Prepare the apricot fruit paste according to the instructions on pages 38–39. Line a 20 x 20 cm (8 x 8 in) shallow tin with plastic wrap or baking parchment and put the paste into the tin to cool.

2 Temper the dark chocolate and spread a thin layer over the paste in the tin. When the chocolate is touch dry, cut into oblong shapes, dipping your knife in water and shaking it between each cut to prevent sticking.

3 Dip each oblong in the remaining tempered dark chocolate so it is fully sealed, then leave to set before cutting away any 'feet' from the chocolate (see page 29).

These superb little logs look and taste really different. They do, however, take quite a while to make. The filling of the logs can also be used to make desserts; try using it to fill filo pastry rolls or whip in some double cream to make an interesting mousse-like dessert. Alternatively, spoon some filling into long-stem glasses, top with crème fraîche and scatter a few nuts on top for decoration.

Apple strudel logs

INGREDIENTS

150 g (5 oz) apple purée, unsweetened

15 g (1/2 oz) sultanas

10 g (1/3 oz) walnuts

zest and juice of 1 lemon

30 g (1 1/4 oz) brown sugar

1/2 teaspoon cinnamon

200 g (7 oz) milk chocolate, chopped or in pellet form

225 g (7 1/2 oz) milk chocolate, chopped or in pellet form, for enrobing

1 Mix the apple purée, sultanas, walnuts, lemon, sugar and cinnamon in a bowl and leave to macerate for at least an hour, longer would be better.

2 Cook the mixture over a low heat, stirring frequently until most of the liquid has evaporated and the mixture is fairly dry. Cool slightly and blitz in a food processor until almost smooth but still with a little texture. Melt 200 g (7 oz) milk chocolate (see page 18), add it to the fruit-and-nut mixture and combine well.

3 Using a piping bag, pipe the mixture into long strips of approximately 1 cm (1/3 in) on a sheet of baking parchment and leave to set.

4 When set, cut into 1.5 cm (1/2 in) logs. Temper the milk chocolate for dipping (see pages 18–21) and using your fingers as for truffles (see page 30), give the logs a thin covering of tempered milk chocolate. Leave to set.

5 When set, give the logs a second, thicker coating with a fairly rough finish, then dust with icing sugar, if wished, before leaving to set.

No recipe book would be complete without a vanilla chocolate. It may seem a little ordinary but chocolate and vanilla is a marriage made in heaven, provided both ingredients are of the best possible quality.

Vanilla chocolates

INGREDIENTS

225 g (7½ oz) white chocolate, chopped or in pellet form, for enrobing

100 ml (3½ fl oz) double cream

150 g (5 oz) milk chocolate, chopped or in pellet form

25 g (1 oz) unsalted butter, softened

seeds from half a vanilla pod

A few drops good-quality vanilla extract

200 g (7 oz) white chocolate, chopped or in pellet form

For white vanilla mice, make as for vanilla chocolates but when you pipe the mounds take a long trail upwards with your nozzle. This will form the nose and must be done quickly before the mix sets. When dipped, place two toasted almond flakes into the chocolate before it sets for the ears and pipe tiny dark chocolate dots for eyes.

1 Temper one-third of the white chocolate for enrobing (see pages 18–21) and spread about a quarter onto a sheet of greaseproof paper. Leave to set. When touch dry, cut out circles from the thin layer of about 1.5 cm (½ in) in diameter.

2 Warm the cream. Add the milk chocolate and stir until all the chocolate is incorporated. If you still have lumps of chocolate, warm the mixture for about 10 seconds in the microwave and stir again until melted.

3 Blend in the butter, vanilla seeds and vanilla extract and whisk until light and smooth. Using a piping bag, pipe small mounds of the ganache onto the white discs of chocolate and leave to set.

4 When set, temper the remaining white chocolate to dip each chocolate to fully seal it. Leave the chocolates to set before cutting away any 'feet' (see page 29).

To avoid disappointment, these should always be made from juicy, homemade crystallized strips of orange peel. No quantities are given in the ingredients list, as they depend on the size of your strips and the number of strips you want to dip. Look at what you have and temper some chocolate. If there isn't enough, you can easily temper some more (and if you have too much, you are sure to find something to do with it!).

Orange sticks

INGREDIENTS

Dark chocolate, chopped or in pellet form

Crystallized strips of orange peel (see pages 36–37)

1 Temper the chocolate (see pages 18–21). Dip the orange strips one at a time into the chocolate using a dipping fork or your fingers to ensure that each strip is fully sealed.

2 Knock off any excess chocolate – you want your orange sticks to have a thin, crisp layer of chocolate. Place on a sheet of baking parchment and leave to set.

For grapefruit sticks, substitute the crystallized orange peel for crystallized grapefruit peel and substitute the dark chocolate for milk chocolate, if wished.

This chocolate is named after the ice cream and looks stunning when cut into. Any remaining fruit paste tastes fantastic dipped in dark chocolate and any remaining ganache can be flavoured and used for truffles.

Neapolitan

INGREDIENTS

For the strawberry paste

150 g (5 oz) strawberries

150 g (5 oz) caster sugar

7.5 g (1/4 oz) powdered pectin

1 tsp tartaric acid dissolved in
   1 tsp water

For the milk chocolate ganache

100 ml (3 1/2 fl oz) cream

200 g (7 oz) milk chocolate in pellets
   or chopped

For the white ganache

100 ml (3 1/2 fl oz) cream

200 g (7 oz) white chocolate in pellets
   or chopped

600 g (1 lb 5 oz) dark chocolate,
   chopped or in pellet form, for
   dipping.

1 Purée the strawberries and make the paste following the method on pages 38–39. Line a deep tin 30 x 30 cm (12 x 12 in) with plastic wrap or baking parchment.

2 To make the milk chocolate ganache, boil the cream, cool it slightly, then pour it over the milk chocolate, stirring well until fully incorporated. Leave the ganache to thicken and cool a little, then pour it into the prepared tin to a depth of 6 mm (1/4 in) and leave to set.

3 When the strawberry paste has cooled, pour it over the milk chocolate ganache, to a depth of 6 mm (1/4 in), and leave to set.

4 Meanwhile, make the white chocolate ganache by boiling the cream, cooling it slightly, then pouring it over the white chocolate, stirring well until fully incorporated. Leave the ganache to thicken and cool a little, then pour it over the fruit paste, to a depth of 6 mm (1/4 in), and leave to set.

5 Temper the dark chocolate (see pages 18–21) and spread a thin layer over the ganache. Leave to set, then cut into cubes.

6 When set, dip each chocolate in the tempered chocolate so it is fully sealed, then leave to set before cutting away any 'feet' from the chocolate (see page 29).

Chocolate and orange always go well together and this recipe is no exception. The crystallized orange peel adds a zing and freshness to the chocolate, as well as making it look stunning.

Orange dessert

INGREDIENTS

2 oranges

8 tsps sugar

40 ml (2 fl oz) water

175 g (6 oz) dark chocolate, chopped or in pellet form, for dipping

65 ml (2½ fl oz) double cream

150 g (5 oz) dark chocolate, chopped or in pellet form

Few drops of orange blossom oil

Few drops of Cointreau or other orange liqueur

1 Using the oranges, sugar and water, prepare the lightly crystallized orange zest (see page 48–49) and dry it out at 100°C (220°F) in the oven, turning once or twice. Store any leftover zest in an airtight container.

2 Temper one-third of the dipping chocolate (see pages 18–21) and spread about a quarter onto a sheet of baking parchment. When touch dry, cut out about 25 circles of 1.5 cm (3/4 in) diameter with a pastry cutter.

3 Warm the cream a little. Add 150 g (5 oz) dark chocolate and stir until all the chocolate is incorporated. If you still have lumps of chocolate, warm the mixture for about 10 seconds in the microwave and stir again. Stir in the orange blossom oil and the Cointreau.

4 Using a piping bag and a 1 cm (1/2 in) nozzle, pipe the ganache onto the dark chocolate circles you have already made and leave to set.

5 When set, temper the remaining dipping chocolate and dip to fully seal. Sprinkle the tops of the chocolates with the crystallized orange zest, then leave to set before cutting away any 'feet' from the chocolate (see page 29).

For orange cups, a rich dessert, make the ganache and spoon it into small glasses or espresso cups. Top with crystallized orange peel (see pages 48–49) and serve with almond tuile biscuits.

These are particularly easy to make. Try varying the fruits and nuts in the clusters and also the type of chocolate used. The clusters should look very irregular so don't try to make them neat.

Pecan-raisin clusters

INGREDIENTS

100 g (3 1/2 oz) dark chocolate, chopped or in pellet form

35 ml (1 1/2 fl oz) double cream

100 g (3 1/2 oz) raisins

100 g (3 1/2 oz) pecans, broken up

200 g (7 oz) dark chocolate, chopped or in pellet form, for dipping

1 Melt 100 g (3 1/2 oz) dark chocolate (see page 18). Add the cream, raisins and pecans and stir well to combine.

2 Put heaped teaspoonfuls of the mixture onto a sheet of baking parchment and leave to set.

3 Temper 200 g (7 oz) dark chocolate (see pages 18–21) and dip each set cluster. Knock off any excess chocolate so the clusters do not become too heavy and leave to set.

For flavoured pecan-raisin clusters before adding the raisins, soak them overnight in a fruit juice of your choice or in alcohol – both Amaretto and Kirsch work well. Drain the raisins well before adding to the mixture.

This chocolate evokes memories of idyllic lazy summer days. Enjoy with a glass of Champagne.

Strawberries and cream

INGREDIENTS

150 g (5 oz) strawberries

150 g (5 oz) sugar

7.5 g (¹/₄ oz) powdered pectin

5 g (¹/₈ oz) tartaric acid dissolved in
   1 tsp water

200 g (7 oz) white chocolate

1 Purée the strawberries and make the paste following the method on pages 38–39.

2 Temper the white chocolate (see pages 18–21) and spread a thin layer over the set paste. When touch dry, cut into squares, dipping your knife in water and shaking it between each cut to prevent sticking. Leave to set completely.

3 When set, dip each chocolate in the remaining tempered white chocolate so it is fully sealed, then leave to set before cutting away any 'feet' from the chocolate (see page 29).

This is a great chocolate for practising a number of your chocolate-making techniques without using a lot of expensive ingredients. As this chocolate is not completely dipped and sealed, it must be eaten within a day or two.

Walnut tower

INGREDIENTS

125 g (4½ oz) white chocolate, chopped or in pellet form

100 ml (3½ fl oz) cream

110 ml (4 fl oz) dark chocolate, chopped or in pellet form

25 g (1 oz) butter

1 tsp vanilla essence

20 walnut halves

1 Temper a third of the white chocolate and spread it onto a sheet of baking parchment so it is about 3 mm (⅛ in) thick. When touch dry, cut out 20 circles of 1.5 cm (¾ in) diameter with a pastry cutter.

2 To make the ganache, boil the cream, allow it to cool a little, then pour it over the dark chocolate, stirring well until all the chocolate is incorporated.

3 Stir in the butter and vanilla essence – the mixture should be warm enough to help melt the butter but it will take a little time and elbow grease to incorporate it fully. Do not pre-melt the butter as this will make the ganache heavy.

4 Using a piping bag and a 1 cm (½ in) nozzle, pipe small mounds of the ganache onto the white discs of chocolate. Put a walnut half on the top of each chocolate and leave to set.

5 Temper the remainder of the white chocolate and dip the bottom two-thirds of each chocolate. Leave to set before cutting away any 'feet' from the chocolate (see page 29).

Dulce de leche is a recipe from Central and South America. It is incredibly easy to make but the method requires patience. Both the praline paste and the gianduja should be bought, as they are fiddly to make.

Dulce de Leche

INGREDIENTS

397 g (14 oz) can condensed milk

50 g (2 oz) praline paste

50 g (2 oz) gianduja

230 g (8 oz) milk chocolate

30 g (1 oz) milk chocolate, chopped or in pellet form, for dipping

Roasted hazelnuts, chopped, to decorate

This recipe should not be made by children, as it can be dangerous if instructions are not followed correctly.

For a simpler chocolate, omit the praline, slice the caramel into squares and dip them in chocolate.

1 Boil the unopened can of condensed milk in a pan of water for 5 hours. Monitor the water level, topping it up regularly to ensure that the can is covered with water at all times.

2 Allow the can to cool to room temperature. The condensed milk will have turned into a thick milk caramel. When back to room temperature, remove the two ends of the can with a can opener and push out the caramel.

3 Temper 200 g (7 oz) of the milk chocolate (see pages 18–21) and spread a thin layer onto a sheet of baking parchment.

4 Melt 30 g (1 oz) milk chocolate, pour it onto the praline and gianduja and stir well to mix. Spread a layer of the praline and gianduja mix onto the chocolate base so it is about 5 mm (1/4 in) thick.

5 Spread a layer of the dulce de leche caramel on top of this and leave to set. When set, cut into diamond shapes, dipping your knife in water and shaking it between each cut to prevent sticking.

6 Temper the milk chocolate for dipping and dip each diamond so that it is fully sealed. Sprinkle the hazelnuts over the chocolate, then leave to set before cutting away any 'feet' from the chocolate (see page 29).

Truffles

Chocolate truffles were originally named after the fungi as, like the fungi, homemade chocolate truffles should look rough and uneven. The truffle is simply a ganache – what goes into the ganache and how it is finished is down to the individual. Truffles can be dipped in chocolate (flavoured or plain) or you can follow tradition and roll your truffles in icing sugar or cocoa, nuts, spices or flavoured sugars.

These truffles have added texture as the biscuits add a bit of crunch. Amaretto truffles taste fantastic when they are first made but they are not a chocolate for keeping. It is common for truffles or ganaches to contain raw egg. This enriches the ganache but also means the truffles must be stored in a fridge and eaten within a week.

Amaretto truffles

INGREDIENTS

100 g (3 1/2 oz) milk chocolate

3 teaspoons double cream

1 egg yolk, lightly beaten

10 g (1/3 oz) butter

2 teaspoons Amaretto or other almond-flavoured liqueur

35 g (1 1/2 fl oz) amaretti biscuits, lightly crushed

100 g (3 1/2 oz) milk chocolate, chopped or in pellet form, for dipping

Note: This recipe contains raw eggs and may be unsuitable for pregnant or nursing mothers, invalids, the elderly, babies and children.

1 Melt 100 g (3 1/2 oz) of the milk chocolate (see page 18). Warm the cream and pour it over the egg yolk. The heat from the cream will help to pasteurize the egg but do take extreme care that you do not boil the cream, as this will cook the egg.

2 Add the butter and Amaretto to the warm cream mixture. Do not melt the butter first, as this will result in a heavy filling. Add the melted chocolate and stir well.

3 Fold the biscuits into the mixture carefully, so as not to break the biscuits further. The biscuits give extra texture to the truffle but they will go soft fairly quickly. Leave to set.

4 When set, scoop out pieces about the size of a walnut and using your finger and thumb, shape into truffles. Don't use the palm of your hand, as this is too warm and will melt the truffle. Leave to set on a sheet of baking parchment.

5 Temper the remainder of the milk chocolate for dipping (see pages 18–21) and roll the truffles around in your chocolate-covered fingers to coat them (see pages 30–31).

6 Roll the truffles in crushed amaretti biscuits, if you wish, then leave to set on a sheet of baking parchment.

The warming cinnamon flavour of the ganache is enhanced by adding cinnamon to the icing sugar used for dusting. Truffles are often enrobed in chocolate before dusting. Use dark chocolate so that the resulting truffle is not too sweet.

Cinnamon truffles

INGREDIENTS

1 clove

1 teaspoon ground cinnamon

70 ml (3 fl oz) double cream

120 g (4 oz) milk chocolate, chopped or in pellet form

120 g (4 oz) dark chocolate, for enrobing

Dusting powder made from 5 percent cinnamon in icing sugar

1 Add the clove and cinnamon to the cream and bring to the boil. Remove the clove. Pour the cream over 120 g (4 oz) of milk chocolate and stir until all the chocolate is incorporated.

2 Using a piping bag, pipe the mixture into quite long lines, about 1.5 cm (3/4 in) in diameter onto a sheet of baking parchment and leave to set. When set, cut the lines into chunks approximately 2 cm (1 in) in length.

3 Temper the dark chocolate (see pages 18–21) and dip each truffle to fully seal it. Immediately after dipping each truffle, roll it in the cinnamon and icing sugar mix, then leave to set.

These are probably the most popular truffles and are nearly always made with Marc de Champagne compound. Champagne truffles were traditionally dusted with icing sugar. White chocolate is often used for dipping, so as not to overpower the Champagne flavour.

Champagne truffles

INGREDIENTS

110 ml (4 fl oz) double cream

100 g (3½ oz) white chocolate, chopped or in pellet form

100g (3½ oz) milk chocolate, chopped or in pellet form

40 g (1½ oz) Marc de Champagne compound

200 g (7 oz) dark chocolate, chopped or in pellet form, for dipping

For brandy and Champagne truffles, replace the milk and white chocolate with dark chocolate and add 2 tsps brandy with the Marc de Champagne. After dipping, roll in icing sugar.

For popping candy and Champagne truffles, replace the milk chocolate with white chocolate and add 1 tsp popping candy when you add the Marc de Champagne. Dip in white chocolate.

1 Boil the cream and leave to cool slightly. Pour the cream over the white and milk chocolate, stirring until all the chocolate is incorporated. Add the Marc de Champagne compound and mix everything together well.

2 Using a piping bag, pipe the mixture into little balls on a sheet of baking parchment and leave to set.

3 Temper the dark chocolate (see pages 18–21) and hand-dip the truffles (see pages 30–31). Leave to set on a sheet of baking parchment.

Cardamom and white chocolate complement each other very well. If you find that using white chocolate in both the filling and the enrobing is too sweet, then replace one or the other with dark chocolate. The addition of a little ground pistachio in the enrobing chocolate diffuses some of the sweetness.

Cardamom truffles

INGREDIENTS

4 cardamom pods

60 ml (2 1/2 fl oz) double cream

100 g (3 1/2 oz) white chocolate, chopped or in pellet form

45 g (1 3/4 oz) salted butter, softened

120 g (4 oz) white chocolate, chopped or in pellet form, for dipping

1 tsp finely powdered pistachios – use either a coffee grinder or put the pistachios into a plastic bag and hit them with a rolling pin

1 Remove the outer skin of the cardamom pods and warm the pods in a low oven for a few minutes. Remove them from the oven and crush with either a rolling pin or a pestle and mortar. Add the cream and bring to the boil. Allow to cool a little.

2 Strain the cream mixture over 100 g (3 1/2 oz) white chocolate, stirring well until all the chocolate is incorporated. Press the cardamom pods with the back of a spoon to release all the flavour. Beat in the butter.

3 Using a piping bag, pipe long lines of the truffle mix about 1.5 cm (3/4 in) in diameter onto a sheet of baking parchment and leave to set. When set, cut into logs about 1.5 cm (3/4 in) long and shape the logs into cardamom pods, if wished. Leave to set again.

4 Temper the remainder of the white chocolate for dipping (see pages 18–21) and mix in the the powdered pistachio. Hand-roll the truffles in the pistachio and white chocolate mixture (see pages 30–31) and leave to set on a sheet of baking parchment.

Moulded chocolates

Chocolate moulds are not really the sort of thing most people have in their kitchen. Don't miss out on this chapter, though, as there are all sorts of things you can use as moulds – jelly moulds, ice cube trays and reusable plastic packaging. Whatever type of mould you use, the same techniques are required. See pages 32–35 for instructions on how to prepare and use moulds.

This recipe will require a little forward planning since the peel takes a few days to prepare. If you have access to a cube-shaped praline mould, use that but if not, use a plastic ice-cube tray as your mould.

Orange and hazelnut cubes

INGREDIENTS

120 g (4 oz) milk chocolate, chopped or in pellet form, for the shells

100 g (3 1/2 oz) milk chocolate, chopped or in pellet form, for the ganache

50 ml (2 fl oz) double cream

20 g (3/4 oz) crystallized peel (see pages 36–37), chopped

20 g (3/4 oz) hazelnuts, roasted and chopped

1 Temper three-quarters of the 120g (4 oz) of milk chocolate (see pages 18–21). Follow steps 1–4 for making moulded chocolates on pages 32–34. Once the chocolate starts to set, tip the mould upside down onto a sheet of baking parchment and leave it to set fully (it may be necessary to put it in a fridge for a short while).

2 Boil the cream, allow it to cool slightly, then pour it over the 100 g (3 1/2 oz) milk chocolate for the ganache. Stir well until the chocolate is fully incorporated.

3 When the chocolate is fully set in the mould, check that it is of a reasonable thickness. It should be crisp and thin so as not to overpower the filling but it must not be so thin that the chocolate falls apart. If necessary apply another coat and repeat step 1.

4 Mix the peel and nuts into the ganache. Using a piping bag, pipe the ganache into the mould, filling each shell almost to the top and leave to set.

5 Temper the remaining quarter of the milk chocolate and use to spread a thin layer over the ganache to seal it. Leave the chocolates to set, then carefully tap them out before cutting away any 'feet' from the chocolates (see page 29).

Chilli and chocolate is a combination that goes back a long way. You would always find chocolate in chilli con carne in Mexico. These days, people often use chilli in chocolate to shock, whereas it should be used simply to enhance the flavour. It is quite easy to get a chilli mould for use with either jelly, chocolate or even ice cubes.

Chilli chocolates

INGREDIENTS

250 g (9 oz) dark chocolate, chopped or in pellet form, for the shells

10 g (1/3 oz) fresh red chillies, chopped (keep and use the seeds)

100 ml (3 1/2 fl oz) double cream

205 g (7 1/4 oz) dark chocolate, chopped or in pellet form, for the ganache

1 Temper 250 g (9 oz) of the dark chocolate (see pages 18–21). Follow steps 1–4 for making moulded chocolates on pages 32–34. Once the chocolate starts to set, tip the mould upside down onto a sheet of baking parchment and leave it to set fully (it may be necessary to put it into a fridge for a short while).

2 Add the chillies to the cream and bring to the boil. Remove from the heat and leave to infuse for 10 minutes. Strain the infusion onto the 205 g (7 1/4 oz) dark chocolate for the ganache and stir well until fully incorporated.

3 When the chocolate is fully set in the mould, check that it is of a reasonable thickness. It should be crisp and thin so as not to overpower the filling but it must not be so thin that the chocolate falls apart. If necessary apply another coat and repeat step 1.

4 Using a piping bag, pipe the ganache into the mould, filling each shell almost to the top and leave to set.

5 Using the tempered chocolate, spread a thin layer over the ganache to seal it. Leave the chocolates to set, then carefully tap them out before cutting away any 'feet' from the chocolates (see page 29).

This chocolate is a little complex but well worth the effort. It's full of lovely English flavours of apples and roses. Rose oil can be bought at delis or specialist foodhalls. Choose the type of apples you buy carefully, as this will determine the sweetness of the finished chocolate.

Rosy English apple

INGREDIENTS

500 g (1 lb) milk chocolate chopped or in pellet form, for the shells

250 ml (8 fl oz) water

200 g (7 oz) sugar

4 drops rose oil

25 ml (1 fl oz) Grand Marnier

275 ml (9 fl oz) well-reduced, unsweetened apple purée

500 g (1 lb) milk chocolate, chopped or in pellet form, for the ganache

200 ml (7 fl oz) double cream

1 Temper 500 g (1 lb) milk chocolate for the shells (see pages 18–21). Follow steps 1–4 for making moulded chocolates on pages 32–34. Once the chocolate starts to set, tip the mould upside down onto a sheet of baking parchment and leave it to set fully (it may be necessary to put it into a fridge for a short while). If you don't have proper chocolate moulds, ice cube trays will work well.

2 Heat the water sufficiently to be able to dissolve the sugar to make a sugar syrup. Add the rose oil, Grand Marnier and apple purée to the syrup and mix well.

3 Warm the cream a little, add 500 g (1 lb) milk chocolate for the ganache and stir until smooth.

4 When the chocolate is fully set in the mould, check that it is of a reasonable thickness. It should be crisp and thin so as not to overpower the filling but it must not be so thin that the chocolate falls apart. If necessary apply another coat and repeat step 1.

5 Using a piping bag, pipe the apple mixture into the mould until each shell is half full and leave to set.

6 Whip the ganache until light and fluffy, then pipe it on top of the apple mixture until the mould is almost full. Leave to set.

7 Using the tempered chocolate, spread a thin layer over the ganache to seal it. Leave the chocolates to set, then carefully tap them out before cutting away any 'feet' from the chocolates (see page 29).

The most difficult part of these is making the cups themselves but the finished product looks great. If you don't have time you can use a chocolate mould or an ice cube mould. Finishing it with the lavender-coloured chocolate adds an elegant touch. Remember to use powder or paste colours, as any water-based colours could cause the chocolate to seize.

Lavender cups

INGREDIENTS

220 g (7½ oz) white chocolate chopped or in pellet form, for the cups

100 ml (3½ fl oz) double cream

1 tsp dried culinary lavender

200 g (7 oz) milk chocolate, chopped or in pellet form, for the ganache

a little lavender colouring (optional)

1 Temper the white chocolate for the cups (see pages 18–21). Paint the inside of some petit fours paper cases with the tempered white chocolate, then leave to dry. Apply a second coat of tempered white chocolate to the inside of each case and leave to dry again.

2 In a pan, bring the cream and culinary lavender to the boil, then allow to cool slightly. Strain the cream onto the milk chocolate and mix well until all the chocolate is incorporated. If necessary warm slightly.

3 Using a piping bag, pipe the mixture into the cups until almost but not completely full. Leave to set. The chocolates can be finished like this but will keep for only a few days.

4 If using, colour a little of the remaining white chocolate and spread it over the ganache, so as to seal each chocolate. Carefully remove the paper cases.

The surprise element in this lovely white chocolate is the presence of the lime jelly. They look best made in a square or oblong praline mould but if you do not have access to a proper mould an ice cube tray will do.

Praline-lime surprise

INGREDIENTS

120 g (4 oz) white chocolate, chopped or in pellet form, for the shells

50 ml (2 fl oz) double cream

15 g (½ oz) praline paste

100 g (3½ oz) white chocolate, chopped or in pellet form, for the ganache

1 tsp Kirsch

Zest and juice of 1½ limes

20 g (1¾ oz) caster sugar

100 ml (3½ fl oz) water

½ leaf gelatine

1 Temper the white chocolate for the shells (see pages 18–21). Follow steps 1–4 for making moulded chocolates on pages 32–34. Once the chocolate starts to set, tip the mould upside down onto a sheet of baking parchment and leave it to set fully (it may be necessary to put it into a fridge for a short while).

2 In a pan, bring the cream to the boil and add the praline paste, stirring until it melts. Add the 100 g (3½ oz) chopped chocolate and stir until fully incorporated. Stir in the Kirsch.

3 Using a piping bag, pipe the mixture into the prepared mould until it is half full.

4 Combine the lime zest, lime juice, sugar and water in a pan. In a separate pan, put the gelatine in to soften in a small quantity of warm water. Squeeze out excess water and add to the lime mixture.

5 Warm the jelly mix gently, allowing the ingredients to combine, then leave to cool. Using a piping bag, pipe the jelly onto the ganache and allow it to set fully.

6 Re-temper the remaining white chocolate for moulding and spread a thin layer over the ganache to seal it. Leave the chocolates to set, then carefully tap them out of the moulds before cutting away any 'feet' from the chocolates (see page 29).

Making the little cups for these chocolates can be frustrating but the effect is amazing! These were among the first chocolates I ever made, long before I ever considered becoming a chocolatier. I made them for dinner parties and they always impressed.

Tipsy coffee cups

INGREDIENTS

100 g (3 1/2 oz) white chocolate, chopped or in pellet form, for the shells

1 tsp good-quality instant coffee

1 tsp warm water

50 g (1 3/4 oz) dark chocolate, chopped or in pellet form

30 ml (1 fl oz) double cream

1 tsp coffee liqueur

1 Temper the white chocolate (see page 18–21) and use it to paint the inside of 12 petit fours paper cases. Leave to dry. Apply a second coat of tempered white chocolate to the inside of each case and leave to dry again.

2 Dissolve the coffee in the warm water. Melt the dark chocolate (see page 18) with the warmed double cream. Mix together the dark chocolate with the dissolved coffee and the coffee liqueur.

3 Using a piping bag, pipe the mixture into the prepared white chocolate cases and leave to set. Carefully remove the paper cases from the chocolates.

Flavoured chocolate

There are times when you need just a little morsel of chocolate. At the end of a large dinner, some really good-quality, thin chocolate is ideal. It doesn't have to be boring, however; exquisitely flavoured thins can be a real treat when served with coffee after a meal. You can add non-water-based flavourings to the chocolate itself or simply decorate the top, which often adds texture. Let your imagination run wild and experiment.

This recipe can be as simple or complex as you wish – the results are discs that just melt in the mouth. These are ideal to serve at the end of a meal or to box and give as a gift. In its simplest form this recipe has only one ingredient – tempered chocolate. The list of possible alternatives, however, is endless.

Basic chocolate thins

INGREDIENTS

Any quantity of chocolate of choice, chopped or in pellet form (see pages 14–15 for information on single-origin and single-estate chocolates, which could help to give your thins an extra edge)

1 Temper the chocolate (see pages 18–21). Drop a teaspoon of the chocolate onto a sheet of cellophane or baking parchment. Alternatively, if you want to make patterned thins, use an acetate transfer sheet (see page 50).

2 Move the back of the spoon in a circular motion to spread the chocolate until it becomes a thin disc, then leave to set. Repeat until you have used all the chocolate.

3 When set, carefully peel the cellophane, baking parchment or acetate away from the chocolate.

For flavoured thins: any ingredients that include water, such as fresh herbs or spices, must be infused in cocoa butter before use. Finely chop or grind 1 1/2 parts fresh herbs or spices and mix into 3 parts melted cocoa butter (for very strong herbs, such as mint, reduce the herb quantity to 1 part). Leave overnight then re-melt and strain. Use the cocoa butter to flavour your chocolate before tempering. One part red pepper to 2 parts cocoa butter can also give a tasty result. Alternatively, flavour the chocolate using an oil, such as mint, orange, lemon or lavender. You could also try decorating your thins with powdered spices, thin slices of stem ginger, crystallized fruits or flowers, berries or nuts.

Tuiles are wafer-thin almond biscuits that get their name from the French for 'tile', after the roof tiles they are meant to resemble. These chocolates are a play on the classic recipe and melt beautifully in the mouth.

Chocolate tuiles

INGREDIENTS

25 g (1 oz) caster sugar

1 tsp water

20 g (¾ oz) crushed almonds

100 g (3½ oz) chocolate of your
choice, chopped or in pellet form

1 Make a light syrup by adding the sugar to the water in a pan and heating gently until the sugar is dissolved. Add the almonds to the syrup and return to the heat. Cook on a low heat until the syrup turns into a light caramel.

2 Add the almonds to the syrup and return to the heat. Cook on a low heat until the syrup turns into a light caramel. Pour the caramel onto a sheet of baking parchment and leave to set into a toffee-like product. When set, crush the toffee into tiny pieces.

3 Temper the chocolate of your choice (see pages 18–21) and mix the toffee pieces into the tempered chocolate.

4 Drop a teaspoon of the mixture onto a small piece of baking parchment – you need a piece of paper for each tuile. Using the back of a teaspoon, spread the mixture into a disc. Slightly drape the parchment over a bowl or rolling pin and leave the tuile to set in a curved shape. When set, peel the paper from the tuile.

Dairy-free chocolates

Although there are more people requiring dairy-free chocolates due to lactose intolerance, these chocolates are delicious whatever your diet. The following recipes contain no cream so the chocolates tend to be light in calories and clean in taste. This chapter includes the entire range of chocolate techniques but you can play around with the recipes – the espresso ganache is used in a truffle, for example, but could be encased in a mould or cut into shapes for dipping.

Coffee has always been a very popular accompaniment to chocolate but recently there has been quite a growth in the use of tea as a ganache flavouring. This recipe can be used with other types of tea but I find that the highly perfumed Chinese teas work best. The water-based ganache suits the very gentle flavour of the tea.

Jasmine and rose

INGREDIENTS

10 g (1/3 oz) jasmine tea

100 ml (3 1/2 fl oz) boiling water

150 g (5 oz) dark chocolate, chopped or in pellet form, for the ganache

Few drops of rose oil

150 g (5 oz) dark chocolate, chopped or in pellet form, for dipping

1 Make a pot of tea using the jasmine tea and the boiling water and leave to stand for two minutes. Measure out 50 ml (2 fl oz) of strained tea and pour it over the dark chocolate for the ganache, stirring well until all the chocolate is incorporated. Add the rose oil and stir well.

2 Line a 20 x 20 cm (8 x 8 in) baking tray with plastic wrap or baking parchment. Spread the ganache into the tray and leave to set.

3 Temper the chocolate for dipping (see pages 18–21). When the ganache is set, spread a thin layer of tempered dark chocolate over the ganache and leave until touch dry. When touch dry, cut into about 25 rectangles and leave to set completely.

4 When completely set, dip each chocolate in the remaining tempered chocolate so it is fully sealed, then leave to set before cutting away any 'feet' from the chocolate (see page 29).

You can make your own marzipan if you wish but there are extremely good marzipans available to buy. In this recipe the marzipan forms the chocolate bases so there is no need to make chocolate circles. The ganache used is the simplest of all water-based ganaches.

Marzipan ganache

INGREDIENTS

100 g (3^{1}/2 oz) marzipan

100 g (3^{1}/2 oz) dark chocolate, chopped or in pellet form, for the ganache, plus a little extra for firming up if necesary

40 ml (2 fl oz) boiling water

110 g (4 oz) dark chocolate, chopped or in pellet form, for dipping

A few toasted almond flakes

Sugar-syrup ganaches
Water-based ganaches usually contain a higher proportion of chocolate to cream-based ganaches to compensate for the extra liquid (much of the liquid in cream is actually fat). This can be modified using a simple syrup (1 part water: 1 part sugar), which extends the shelf life, adds a little more flavour but also makes the ganache sweeter so your choice of recipe is ultimately down to your personal taste.

1 Roll out the marzipan to a thickness of 4 mm (^{1}/8 in). Using a 1.5 cm (^{3}/4 in) round pastry cutter, cut out approximately 20 marzipan circles.

2 Pour the boiling water over the chocolate for the ganache and stir well until fully incorporated. Allow the ganache to firm up a little. If the chocolate seems too soft, add a little extra melted chocolate and stir well.

3 Using a piping bag, pipe mounds of ganache about 1 cm (^{1}/2 in) high onto the marzipan circles and leave to set.

4 Temper the chocolate for dipping (see pages 18–21) and dip each chocolate so it is fully sealed. Decorate immediately with almond flakes, then leave to set before cutting away any 'feet' from the chocolate (see page 29).

If you don't have any espresso to hand, you can still make these truffles by using strong, good-quality instant coffee but do not use coffee essence, as this produces a very artificial taste nothing like real coffee.

Espresso truffle

INGREDIENTS

50 ml (2 fl oz) double-strength
   fresh espresso

100 ml (3¹/2 fl oz) dark chocolate,
   chopped or in pellet form, for
   the ganache

120 g (4 oz) dark chocolate, chopped
   or in pellet form, for dipping

1 Pour the warm espresso over the chocolate for the ganache and stir well until the chocolate is fully incorporated.

2 Make a piping bag out of baking parchment (see pages 42–43) and fill it with the ganache. Pipe small mounds of ganache onto baking parchment and leave to set.

3 Using your finger and thumb, shape the mounds into balls – avoid using the palm of your hand, as it is warmer than your fingers and could melt the chocolate. Leave to set.

4 Temper the dark chocolate for dipping (see pages 18–21) and dip each chocolate so it is fully sealed. Leave to set before cutting away any 'feet' from the chocolate (see page 29).

Although orange and cinnamon make a lovely Christmas chocolate, once you've tasted these you'll want to eat them all year round.

Orange and cinnamon

INGREDIENTS

1 cinnamon stick

350 ml (12 fl oz) orange juice

200 g (7 oz) dark chocolate, chopped or in pellet form, for the ganache

200 g (7 oz) dark chocolate, for dipping

crystallized orange peel, sliced, for decoration (see pages 36–37)

1 Put the cinnamon and orange juice in a pan and boil until the liquid is reduced by a fifth (about 70 ml/3 fl oz). Remove the cinnamon stick and allow to cool slightly. Pour the reduced juice over the chocolate for the ganache and stir well until the chocolate is fully incorporated.

2 Line a 20 x 20 cm (8 x 8 in) baking tray with plastic wrap or baking parchment. Spread the ganache into the prepared tray and leave to set until firm.

3 Temper the chocolate for dipping (see pages 18–21). When the ganache is set, spread a thin layer of tempered dark chocolate over the ganache and leave until touch dry. Cut into diamond shapes and leave to set completely.

4 When completely set, dip each chocolate in the remaining tempered chocolate so it is fully sealed, then immediately add the orange peel as decoration. Leave to set before cutting away any 'feet' from the chocolate (see page 29).

This is a really lovely chocolate, based on the well-known Cosmopolitan cocktail with its fruity cranberry flavour and vodka kick. If you're lacking equipment or inspiration for moulds to make this chocolate, you could try making it as a dipped chocolate instead.

Cosmopolitan

INGREDIENTS

70 g (2¹/2 oz) dark chocolate, chopped or in pellet form, for the shell

350 ml (12 fl oz) cranberry juice

200 g (7 oz) dark chocolate, chopped or in pellet form, for the ganache

30 ml (1 fl oz) vodka

1 Temper the dark chocolate for the shell (see pages 18–21). Follow steps 1–4 for making moulded chocolates on pages 32–34. Once the chocolate starts to set, tip the mould upside down onto a sheet of baking parchment and leave it to set fully (it may be necessary to put it into a fridge for a short while).

2 Put the cranberry juice in a pan and boil until reduced in volume by a fifth to give a strong, rich flavour. Leave the juice to cool a little. Pour the reduced, cooled cranberry juice over the chocolate for the ganache and stir well until fully incorporated. Add the vodka and mix in well – as well as adding flavour this also acts as a preservative.

3 Make a piping bag out of baking parchment (see pages 42–43) and fill it with the ganache. Pipe the ganache into the mould, filling each shell almost to the top and leave to set.

4 Using the remaining tempered chocolate, spread a thin layer over the ganache to seal it. Leave the chocolates to set, then carefully tap them out before cutting away any 'feet' from the chocolates (see page 29).

Chocolate and children

Children love creating things – as well as making a mess. Chocolate is a relatively safe way of introducing a child to cooking, as it melts at a low temperature and is a low-risk food. All the chocolate in these recipes must be tempered so if your child has the patience, tempering can be part of the fun. You may want to temper the chocolate yourself first, however, and jump straight to the creative bits together. Experiment with flavours and colours.

Your child will be delighted by these colourful creations. The major advantage is that they are thin but look quite big, so when the children get around to devouring them, they won't be eating too much chocolate. These thins also make lovely little gifts if arranged nicely on a plate or in a small box, ideal to give to grandma or auntie.

Playful thins

INGREDIENTS

Any amount of dark, milk or white chocolate, chopped or in pellet form

Small sweets

Raisins

1 Temper the chocolate (see pages 18–21). Take a teaspoonful of the tempered chocolate and drop it onto a sheet of baking parchment. Move the back of a spoon in a circular motion to spread the chocolate until it becomes a thin disc about 3 cm (1 1/4 in) in diameter, then leave to set. Even tiny children can do this – show them first and then let them do it. It really does not matter how circular the circle is or exactly what size it ends up.

2 While the chocolate is still wet, decorate it with sweets and raisins. Leave the chocolate thin to dry while you make the next one. Do not do lots of thins at once and then decorate them, as they are likely to go dry and then the decoration will not stick.

3 When the thins are dry, peel away the parchment. Small children may require help with this bit.

The trick with this recipe is to spread fairly small quantities of chocolate at a time so that it doesn't set before you can cut out all your shapes. These tasty little treats will delight any child and they are so easy to make.

Yummy chocolate shapes

INGREDIENTS

Any quantity of dark, milk or white chocolate, chopped or in pellet form

Small sweets for decoration

1 Temper the chocolate (see pages 18–21). Pour some of this tempered chocolate onto a sheet of baking parchment and spread it with a spatula or pallet knife until it is smooth and of uniform thickness (about 5 mm/1/4 in). Leave until it is firm to the touch but not completely set.

2 While the chocolate sets, make sure your biscuit cutters are clean and dry and, if possible, a little shiny, as this will make it easier to cut the chocolate. Then simply cut out your fun shapes – bears, gingerbread people and stars are a suggestion.

3 You can stick on a few sweets to decorate the shapes using a little left-over chocolate as glue. Really young children love putting on eyes, buttons and so on.

This recipe involves piping and a knife so is probably only suitable for children over 8 years old. Gather together a collection of colourful sweets to use as decoration.

Chocolate wands

INGREDIENTS

Any quantity of dark, milk or white chocolate, chopped or in pellet form

Roasted, chopped nuts of choice

Tiny brightly coloured sweets

Marshmallows, chopped

1 Get children to try making their own piping bags from baking parchment (see pages 42–43) – it is just like origami! Be prepared to help them out, however, if they find it a bit tricky.

2 Temper the chocolate (see pages 18–21) and half-fill one piping bag for each child. Cut a reasonable-sized hole in the end of each bag, then pipe long lines of chocolate about 1 cm (1/2 in) thick onto a sheet of baking parchment.

3 While the chocolate is still liquid, scatter all the other ingredients over them in whatever design you prefer and leave to set completely. Perhaps make wands with another colour chocolate while you wait.

4 When the chocolate is set, cut your wands into whatever size you like. These are great to eat as they are or you could tie a pretty ribbon around them and give them as a gift. Alternatively, stick one in an ice cream.

It is not necessary for the chocolate to be tempered in this recipe but you can do so if you want to practise the technique. These balls are light and you can experiment with adding other ingredients of your choice.

Chocolate crispy balls

INGREDIENTS

Any quantity of dark, milk or white chocolate, chopped or in pellet form

Toasted rice cereal

Raisins

Glacé cherries, chopped

1 Melt the chocolate (see page 18) then add the cereal and raisins to it. The proportions are totally down to taste – more cereal will make the chocolates lighter. Add the chopped cherries to give extra colour, if you like.

2 Form the mixture into small, walnut-sized balls and put each ball into a petit fours or sweet paper case. Leave to set. These clusters are really adaptable so try experimenting with different ingredients to add to the chocolate, such as honeycomb or marshmallows.

Again, it is not necessary for the chocolate to be tempered in this recipe. These truffles really are child's play and they can be made by very young children. They make an ideal gift for granny when presented in a pretty little box.

Children's truffles

INGREDIENTS

100 g (3¹/2 oz) slightly stale cake

100 g (3¹/2 oz) milk chocolate, chopped or in pellet form

25 g (1 oz) raisins

75 ml (3 fl oz) double cream

Cocoa or icing sugar for rolling

1 Crumble the cake into crumbs. Melt the chocolate (see page 18). Add the crumbed cake and other ingredients to the melted chocolate and mix well with a large spoon.

2 Use your fingers to make small rounds of the mixture and place each one on a sheet of baking parchment.

3 Put some cocoa powder or icing sugar on a plate and gently coat the truffles using just your finger and thumb to roll them. Do not use the palm of your hand as this is warm and will cause the truffles to melt.

4 Place the truffles back onto the baking parchment and leave them to set completely.

For this recipe you will need a shallow, round mould. The plastic trays that cream containers come in at the supermarket are perfect and supermarkets will usually quite happily give you them for free.

Chocolate faces

INGREDIENTS

Any quantity of dark, milk or white chocolate, chopped or in pellet form

Sweets

Raisins

Flaked almonds

1 Polish the tray with some kitchen towel so that it is clean and the chocolate will come away easily. Temper the chocolate (see pages 18–21) and pour it into the circular bases in the tray to a depth of about 5 mm ($1/4$ in).

2 Carefully bang the tray on a table three times to remove any air bubbles. Leave to set for about 20 minutes in a cool place (but not the fridge).

3 When set, the chocolate should have shrunk away from the base and you should easily be able to tap out the shapes onto a clean, dry surface. Some cream trays have a crinkly surface, which gives a lovely texture to the chocolate face.

4 Decorate the face using sweets, raisins or almonds using a little leftover tempered chocolate as glue.

For Santa faces, add a red hat cut out of red ready-made fondant icing and a beard made out of white ready-made fondant icing.

For chocolate medals, cut a small slot near the top of the disc with a knife so you can slot a ribbon through.

Children love making chocolate models. You can buy proper moulds from kitchen shops or online but you will be surprised at what you can find at home. The moulds need to be plastic (for ease of use), clean, dry and, if possible, shiny. Moulds for ice cubes or jelly work really well, but you can also use packaging. Sweets sometimes come in shaped plastic containers, which make good moulds. Bases of plastic water bottles can be used to make chocolate tubs that can be decorated with sweets or older children could pipe a message on them.

Modelling

INGREDIENTS

Any amount of white chocolate, chopped or in pellet form

Powder or paste colour(s) of choice

Any quantity of milk chocolate, chopped or in pellet form

1 Polish the inside of your chosen mould with kitchen paper. Temper the white chocolate (see pages 18–21) and colour it either one colour or separate it into bowls for more than one colour (see page 55).

2 Ask the child to use clean, dry fingers to put some detail into his or her mould using the tempered white or coloured chocolate. This could be facial features, squiggles or anything else they choose.

3 Ask the child to wave the mould around in the air to encourage the chocolate to set.

4 Temper the milk chocolate and using a finger put a thin layer of tempered chocolate all over the inside of the mould and the decoration. You need to make sure you do not leave any gaps, otherwise the finished article will have holes. Leave to set.

5 Next, pour tempered milk chocolate from the bowl to fill the mould to the top. Always keep a gap of about 15 cm (6 in) between the bowl and the mould, as this makes pouring so much easier – it also looks more fun. Alternatively, spoon the chocolate into the mould.

6 Tap the mould on a table three times to ensure that the chocolate has got into every little crevice and also to remove any air bubbles.

7 Pour the excess chocolate back into the bowl – figures need to be hollow unless they are very small, in which case you can leave the mould to set full. Tap the edge of the mould to ensure as much chocolate as possible ends up in the bowl. You need the shell to be about 3–4 mm ($^1/_4$ in) thick. If it is a very large mould it needs to be a little thicker.

8 Leave the chocolate to firm up, then remove any excess chocolate by running your finger around the edge of the mould. Then place the mould in the fridge for about 15 minutes to set fully.

9 Remove the mould from the fridge. You should see that the chocolate has shrunk away from the edges and it can now be tapped out onto a clean surface.

10 You can decorate the model further, if you wish. Use a piping bag or stick on sweets using a little melted chocolate as glue.

About Auberge du Chocolat

I have always loved eating good-quality chocolate and have enjoyed experimenting with it. From as far back as I can remember I have made chocolates for friends and special occasions, but in 2005 my husband and I decided to open a chocolatier dedicated to quality chocolate. We called it 'Auberge du Chocolat'.

The aim of this artisan family business is simple – to get everyone passionate about chocolate by offering sublime chocolates. In order to achieve this all our products are handmade using blends of the finest ingredients. In 2009, our son Jonathan decided to relaunch our signature range of chocolates, giving them a more contemporary feel. In keeping with the current Japanese influence on chocolate, he came up with Sesame and Wasabi. Some of the more traditional flavours were also given a new angle, like Strawberry and Balsamic. A really exciting aspect of this relaunch was the introduction of some delicious dairy-free chocolates, some of which you'll find in this book.

Our original shop in Gerrards Cross used to be a shoe shop and over our first Christmas period we were asked so often for shoes that we decided to make chocolate ones. Our wide range of amazing stilettos has now become really well-known! Since then we have had many commissions for unusual chocolate models, from battleships to bouquets.

While chocolate is popular all year round for gifts and wedding favours, less is eaten during the summer months, so in 2006 we expanded into ice cream gelato. Now we also make fudge the old-fashioned way with natural ingredients.

A good way to enthuse people about chocolate is to get them to make it themselves so we run workshops, courses and parties for all ages and abilities. Auberge also reaches out into the local community by working with schools and social groups. Corporate groups also enjoy team-building with us.

By 2009 it became clear that the Gerrards Cross shop alone was no longer big enough, so at Easter 2010 we moved our production into Chesham while still retaining the original shop at Gerrards Cross. We also opened our Chocolate Academy at the Chesham site, enabling us to reach out to even more people.

We have always been keen to operate our business in an ethical way, sourcing fairly traded and organic ingredients where possible.

Recognition of our work has come from the many awards we have won from the Academy of Chocolate, the Great Taste Awards and the Ice Cream Alliance. Our son Jonathan received his first chocolate award at age 17 (from the Academy of Chocolate) and continues to add to his tally.

We love sharing our ideas and recipes so follow us on our website www.aubergechocolat.co.uk, Facebook, YouTube or Linkedin. I hope you will share in our passion.

Anne Scott

Index

Acknowledgements

I would like to thank my husband, Ian, for patiently reading through all of this and for tasting numerous recipes. I also thank my son, Jonathan, for allowing me to use some of his recipes and my two daughters, Sarah and Rachael, for all their help and support.

Picture Credits